The Battered Wife
And Her Five Little Kids All Dressed In White

The Battered Wife
And Her Five Little Kids
All Dressed In White

GEORGE GARRIGUES

City Desk Publishing

© 2019 George Garrigues

All rights reserved. No part of this publication may be reproduced, distributed, or transmitted in any form or by any means, including photocopying, recording, or other electronic or mechanical methods, without the prior written permission of the publisher, except in the case of brief quotations embodied in critical reviews and certain other noncommercial uses permitted by copyright law.

The images in this book are included in the copyright, having been modified and edited from originals in the public domain, or as fair use.

City Desk Publishing, 480 Morro Avenue, Suite E, Morro Bay, CA 93442

For permission requests, write to the publisher at the address above.

Printed in the United States of America

Other works by
George Garrigues

- *He Usually Lived With a Female*
- *Los Angeles's The Palms Neighborhood*
- *Mrs. Hartley and the Senator*
- *Mrs. Dodge and the House Painter*
- *Dora Doxey and the Doctor*
- *The Shyster Lawyer*
- *Marguerite Martyn: America's Forgotten Journalist*
- *Liberty Bonds and Bayonets*

   (and too many newspaper articles to count)

Contents

	Foreword	1
1.	The Pacific	5
2.	The Killing	10
3.	The Arrest	21
4.	The Funeral	27
5.	Summer 1916	32
6.	The First Trial	39
7.	Autumn 1916	70
8.	Beer Fountains and Votes for Women	81
9.	Freeholder Ryman	87
10.	The Second Trial	99
11.	The Verdict	113
12.	Observations	119
13.	Afterword	128
	Chronology	139

Foreword

It was pitch dark outside a stately New Jersey mansion early in the morning of Tuesday, July 11, 1916. Inside, Christof Beutinger's body lay on the floor, and Margaret Claire Beutinger held a smoking gun.

Two little girls crept from their bed and clung to their mother. She arose with the revolver carefully pointed away from them, and then, in fright, threw it down. She sank back and wept. Six-year-old Marie ran to soak a towel in water from the sink and returned to bathe her mother's face. The servants came.

Was it murder or self-defense?

I unfold this tale as almost everybody learned it at that time — through the witnessing of the newspaper reporters who saw these events in person, or who interviewed people who had.

These are real articles from real newspapers of the era, but I have edited them for you, today's reader — yet always with the knowledge that I must not play false with you. (Occasionally some quaint phrasings from the past sneak in; you will recognize them when you see them.) The stories are all dated and identified so you can check the originals for yourself. For newspapers outside the Continental United States — Hawaii and Jamaica — the dates of publication may be several days after the actual event.

Sometimes the reporters got the facts wrong, or they misinterpreted them. Often one reporter saw or heard one thing and the reporter at his or her side saw or heard something really quite different.

Seldom in those days were reporters given bylines, but when they were — just twice — I included them.

• • •

There was a smoking gun and the smell of gunpowder, and, no doubt about it, five bullets were in Christof Beutinger's body. Blood drenched the floor.

How did it all begin?

The story started in Jamaica, in the West Indies, which in those days was a British colony. Most of the people who lived on that island just south of Cuba were of black African descent, but all those in charge and who ran things and made most of the money were white, and they had come from England, or were descended from English colonists.

Jamaica was where Margaret Claire was born. Her father, George Abrahams, was English — a judge, as a matter of fact. His brother was Lord Devore of Kent, England, and they were cousins of the banking Rothschilds.

Margaret Claire Beutinger's birth name was Abrahams. Her family was Jewish. At some point, she became a Roman Catholic. Often her name was spelled Clair.

The man whose body lay on the floor was Christof, or Christopher, Beutinger. His family was German. Undoubtedly Lutheran. Margaret and Christof may have met in London. Or on a voyage from New York. Or in Jamaica, where she was introduced to him, "big, jovial, and good-natured"; the stories differed. They were married in 1906 or 1907, in Kingston, the capital city of Jamaica, when she was in her late teens.

During her trial for murder, if you had been around in 1916, you could have read about—

A WIFE'S EMOTION

Saturday, 7/12/1916 *(New York Herald)*. After a brief residence in New York, the couple went to the Philippines, where Beutinger was a clerk in the quartermaster's office.

Even then, in their first married year, he struck and abused her. Her husband took to drink and gambling and lost large sums of money. When she complained, he beat her worse than ever. He kicked her at times when her physical condition was delicate.

"But you loved him?" she was asked.

"Yes, there never was a time when I did not love him," she replied.

She made those statements while on trial for her life.

The prosecuting attorney in Essex County, New Jersey, did not think that firing five bullets into a man was a good idea. In fact, he believed it was a crime. He thought that Margaret should have run away instead of pointing a loaded gun and pulling a trigger. That was the law in New Jersey.

So Mrs. Beutinger was taken to court, charged with first-degree murder, and the ultimate penalty could be death.

1. The Pacific

In 1898 the United States became a Pacific Ocean power when it took the Philippine Islands from Spain and absorbed Hawaii. Both countries became U.S. territories, and of course the government had to send people to staff these new bureaucracies. One of them was Christof Beutinger

In 1905 and 1909, the Official Register of the United States listed Christof Beutinger as a clerk in the War Department, with a government salary to match.

Margaret Claire, the young bride, went with him to the Philippines. Very soon she found that Christof was a heavy drinker. And a bit later she discovered that he was making shady deals with Japanese businessmen.

Time passed, and they had babies, but by 1914 the gov-

ernment had had enough of Christof Beutinger's shenanigans and sent him packing. He and Margaret sailed for the United States.

Passenger travel could be by luxury liner, or on a freighter, or in a U.S. Army transport or a naval vessel. One notable stopping point for ocean travelers was the famed Moana Hotel in Honolulu (pictured, previous page). And the Moana was hopping. Most nights you could dance to a jazz band, with well-off locals and tourists mingling, drinking, and having fun. The Beutingers — now with little children — stopped there on their way back to the Mainland.

It was at the Moana that Claire Beutinger decided to call it quits with the marriage because — well, read on.

WOMAN TO DIVORCE THIS BRUTE

Monday, 6/8/1914 (*Honolulu Star-Bulletin*). Christopher Beutinger, a civilian employee identified with the Philippines insular government, was thwarted Saturday in the abuse of his wife, Margaret Claire, by police and others who hastened to answer her cries for assistance in the Moana Hotel.

Beutinger, when finally subdued, was arrested through the intervention of the woman's attorney, W.R. Rawlins, who was in the hallway outside the couple's room.

Beutinger, who had been drinking, resisted mightily, but he was subdued by mounted Police Officer Fred Wright and Sergeant Fred Iaukea.

AND HER FIVE LITTLE KIDS ALL DRESSED IN WHITE

He spent some dozen hours at the police station, and he was definitely the wealthiest prisoner lodged in the municipal bastille for quite some time. Officers temporarily relieved him of money, checks, drafts, and other forms of wealth to the value of more than $12,000, apparently the accumulation of several years' residence in Manila. *(Pretty good, for a government worker.)*

When Mrs. Beutinger showed up the next day at the station, she told officers she had suffered violent abuse at his hands for about five years.

Before departing for California as a passenger in a United States Army transport yesterday morning, Mrs. Beutinger took steps to secure a divorce from her husband, alleging cruel and inhuman treatment.

She consulted an attorney who told her he could do nothing for her because she was not a resident of Hawaii.

She continued her voyage on to San Francisco in the U.S. Army transport *Sheridan*, but her husband was advised to take up his journey by some other means, and he chose the Pacific Mail liner *Siberia (next page)*.

Almost two years later, Iaukea, who had been promoted to captain, still recalled the incident.

SCREAMS AT THE MOANA HOTEL

Wednesday, 2/14/1917 *(Honolulu Star-Bulletin)*. Police Captain Fred Iaukea has given a brief story of the episode with Beutinger. He said:

"Beutinger was extremely jealous, and one Saturday night the man dragged his wife roughly off the dance floor and took her upstairs to their room.

"Attorney William Rawlins was in the hall, and he heard a terrified scream. He and policeman Fred Wright opened the door to their room, found Beutinger beating his wife, and called for me. I went in the patrol wagon and brought him to the jail.

"He was a massive fellow, larger than me, and inclined to be impertinent. I allowed him considerable liberty in jail at first, but later locked him in a cell when he got too saucy. I thought I was going to have to fight him.

"The next afternoon his wife came to the station and

pleaded for his release, but Beutinger would have nothing to do with her, saying he was finished with her.

"She refused to press the charge of assault, and after he promised to take care of her and go on to the States — she would have been destitute if he hadn't — I released him. They left on separate ships."

Mrs. Beutinger told Iaukea that her husband had been chief clerk in the quartermaster's department in Manila and had been discharged for grafting, but was reinstated after she made a trip to Washington, D.C., to use her influence with officials there.

For a similar offense he was discharged a second time, the woman told the officer.

2. The Killing

WIFE KILLS WEALTHY HUSBAND

Wednesday, 7/12/1916 *(The New York Times)*. Christopher Beutinger, a wealthy representative of coal exporters at 1 Broadway, was shot to death about 4 o'clock this morning by his wife, the police say. His body was found in her bedroom in the Westover section of Caldwell, New Jersey.

His wife, Margaret, said she had fired five shots, straight at him.

The couple had five children, ranging in age from three to nine. The children and a servant, John Cummings of Yonkers, were awakened by the pistol shots. When Cummings entered Mrs. Beutinger's room, her husband was dead. Both were in their night garments.

The shooting was the climax of weeks of bitter quarreling. Caldwell Police Chief John Harkey said the wife had called him to the house last Thursday to acquaint him with the situation, saying "something" would happen and complaining bitterly of cruel and brutal treatment by her husband.

The husband came to his wife's bedroom about 4 a.m. and demanded admittance; she told him to leave, but he refused to do so. She then drew a pistol from under her pillow and shot him.

> ## BEUTINGER KILLED IN WIFE'S BEDROOM
>
> Culmination of Long Series of Quarrels in Ex-Army Officer's Household.
>
> ### MRS. BEUTINGER IN JAIL
>
> Had Complained to Police of Coal Exporter's Cruelty — Fired Five Shots, She Said.
>
> *Special to The New York Times.*
>
> CALDWELL, N. J., July 11.—Christopher Beutinger, a wealthy representative of coal exporters at 1 Broadway, was shot to death about 4 o'clock this morning by his wife, the police say. His

At about 6 a.m., Harkey received a telephone call from an excited servant exclaiming there had been a murder at the Beutingers'.

"When I got the message," the chief said, "I thought

sure, from what she had told me earlier, that it was the wife who had been murdered."

Harkey arrived at the house at the same time as a doctor who had also been called. Mrs. Beutinger was in the library surrounded by her children. They will probably be sent temporarily to the New Hope Convent, where the little girls have been cared for from time to time.

The Beutingers occupied a fine residence in Caldwell, for which they are said to have paid $25,000 about four months ago, but they are not well known there. Still, many people had heard of their domestic difficulties.

Dr. E.S. Ives of Little Falls has been treating Mrs. Beutinger for minor injuries that she attributed to her husband, one of them a wound to her eye which still showed traces of discoloration.

Police say Mrs. Beutinger had been in William Starck's drugstore near her home last Friday and told Starck that there would soon be some "great excitement" in the neighborhood. She asked the druggist where she could get a good lawyer, and the same day she retained Walter Brandley, a member of the Caldwell Common Council.

Mrs. Beutinger is a handsome and intelligent woman of the Spanish type. She is 28; her husband was 42.

Beutinger is said to have done well as a wholesale coal dealer and exporter, representing several important mining properties and amassing a considerable fortune. It was said last night by one who knew Beutinger in Manila that he left the service under a cloud, resulting from a coal scandal in which a contract was awarded to a Japanese firm from which he had received several thousand dollars.

After this scandal, the family left the Philippines and went to Honolulu, where he was arrested on a charge of wife-beating, but she refused to press charges.

The couple separated about six years ago, but subsequently tried to live together again. They moved to Mount Vernon, New York, where their youngest son was born. Then they moved to Caldwell.

RECEIVED A REVOLVER BY EXPRESS

Wednesday, 7/12/1916 (*New York Sun*). To John Cummings, her gardener, who was the first one to enter the room, she said:

"I have finished him this time. He won't bother me any more."

Beutinger's body lay on the floor. One bullet struck him behind the ear and pierced his brain, and four others entered his head and chest as he staggered and fell.

When Police Chief Harkey and Dr. George B. Verbeck arrived, they found Mrs. Beutinger lying across her bed and her five children about her; she was crying hysterically that she knew she had done wrong.

They moved to Caldwell four months ago and bought the former home of Caldwell notable Fillmore Condit at 7 Hillcrest Road. Here their quarrels broke out afresh; last Wednesday there was a dispute over a child's doll, and, according to Mrs. Beutinger and her lawyer, her husband tried to gouge out his wife's eyes with his thumbs.

She ordered a revolver and a box of cartridges from New York, which she received by express and hid in a dresser drawer.

Last night the couple had another altercation in the suite where she slept with her three sons, Frederick, 7; Christopher Jr., or Charlie, 4, and William, 3, and two daughters, Margaret, 8, and Marie, 5.

Her husband came to his wife's room twice and left each time after she ordered him out. The third time, he seized her, and, fearing bodily harm, she drew the revolver from beneath her pillow and shot him as he sat in a chair. He arose, and she fired four more times.

Gardener Cummings ran to the room, then aroused the caretakers, Eugene Graaf and his wife, and told them to call the police. He returned and tried to soothe the children.

CHILDREN PLAY AT HOME

Wednesday, 7/12/1916 *(New York Tribune)*. Yesterday afternoon the five fatherless Beutinger children *(pictured)* were picking cherries in their playground-dooryard when a reporter visited the neighborhood. They are too young to realize the significance of their mother's remark: "I killed him for the sake of my children — it is better they should never know how he abused me."

Revolver shots aroused Margaret, age 8, and Marie,

two years younger, from their sleep in their big brass bedstead. They were unmoved by questions about the tragedy.

"I didn't see what Mama had done to Papa," Margaret said. "But I did cry when he struck Mama before she fired the gun."

Three-year-old William, the youngest child, is said by the neighbors to be the image of his father. Frederick and Charles, his older brothers, played games, rode their bicycles around the lawn, and climbed the cherry trees as if nothing had happened.

Charles was also known as Christof or Christopher Jr., and later as Peter.

It is expected that the children will be sent to the Mount Hope Convent School, near Yonkers.

THE BATTERED WIFE

"Within a month after we came here, they began to quarrel again," recalled Mrs. Louise Graaf. She and her husband, Eugene, the caretakers, are temporarily taking care of the children.

She recalled:

"He was mean to her. He nagged her all the time. Yesterday she told me she feared he would be abusive when he came home because he had been celebrating with his German friends the arrival of the submarine at Baltimore."

The German u-boat Deutschland, the largest undersea vessel made to that time, visited Baltimore harbor after sneaking undetected through the English Channel and transiting the Atlantic during the second year of the European War. (Captain Paul L. Koenig and some of the crew are pictured in Baltimore with a visitor.)

Mrs. Graaf continued:

"He telephoned that he would not be home to dinner. That was nothing unusual. But he came at 7 o'clock last night, and I had to get his dinner ready in a hurry.

"While he was eating, Mrs. Beutinger came down to the kitchen and told me that he had threatened to kill her and that she was afraid that he was going insane, as his brother did.

"But we never knew that she had sent to New York for a revolver, which came by express Monday."

The housekeeper went on:

"I was awakened at 5 a.m. by the shots. Gene and I ran downstairs to her room, right under ours.

"He lay on the floor near her bed, dead, with blood flowing from a wound behind his ear. There were three other wounds around his heart and one in his right arm. Mrs. Beutinger stood looking at the empty revolver on her bureau. She was calm; she did not weep; she seemed to be content with herself."

KILLS HER WEALTHY HUSBAND

Wednesday, 7/12/1916 (*New York Herald*). When pressed to reveal causes that led to the tragedy, Mrs. Beutinger said:

"In the nine years we were married, I bore him seven children, five of whom survive. I divorced him once for consorting with other women, but we were married again on the promise of his reform and to give my children a father. Since then, he has driven several women servants from my home; and after trying to kill me last Wednesday night, he came into my room this morning, and I shot him because he seized me by the throat and would have choked me.

"Secondarily, he was an ardent German, and perhaps I never could forget that I am an Englishwoman."

Beutinger's vigor made him a worker, and he required little sleep or rest. Among his acquaintances he was known as a businessman of much ability, and he had the reputation of being a difficult man with whom to bargain.

About nine years ago, Mrs. Beutinger, then still Miss Abrahams, was in London when Beutinger was in that city as a purchasing agent for the U.S. government in the Philippines. They met in that city, were married, and went to Manila to live. There the two eldest girls were born.

The family came to New York City, and Beutinger established himself as a commission agent for coal mines and is said to have amassed a fortune between $500,000 and $1 million. They purchased a home at 28 Clinton Place in the Chester Hill section of Mount Vernon, but did not live happily there.

It was there that twins were born, and there they died. Trouble between husband and wife was constant. Following the birth of Willie, two years ago, Mrs. Beutinger obtained a divorce. Her testimony mentioned several women, and other witnesses testified that Beutinger was acquainted with many women.

She went to Jamaica, and Beutinger followed her,

swearing to be a better husband. They remarried in Kingston. She refused to return to Mount Vernon, where her twins had died, so they purchased an estate in Caldwell from Fillmore Condit, vice president of the California Oil Company, in Mrs. Beutinger's name. The large, modern, country house is surrounded by three acres, and the place has a magnificent view down a long and beautiful valley.

She said several servants left because of him, and one of them charged that he had molested her.

When Beutinger got home on Wednesday night, there was a quarrel because dinner had not been kept for him. After he had eaten, he saw Marie playing with a new doll, and he grabbed it and tried to make it stand on its own feet.

"I told him to be careful, that he might break the doll's legs," she said. "He flew into a rage, leaped upon me and tried to gouge my eye out with his thumb. He beat me until the servants intervened.

"The following day, Thursday, I went to Chief of Police John Harkey and asked him what was the best thing to do. I told him I was afraid of my husband and knew that if I left him or had him arrested, he would kill me, as he often said he would do. The chief said he would not interfere in family troubles but advised me to see a lawyer, and upon my request he recommended Walter G. Brandley."

Lawyer Brandley said yesterday he had been arranging for her and the children to enter a retreat where Beutinger could not find them, and then he would begin a legal action for a separation.

Since Wednesday night the couple had occupied separate bedrooms, hardly speaking to each other. The wife said he woke her twice early Thursday morning, and she ordered him out twice. He came in a third time, "drew a chair up to the bed, and sat down."

"He made demands that made me hate him more than ever. I told him I hated him, and I had my hand on the pistol under the pillow. He sprang upon me and tried to choke me. Then I drew the pistol and fired one shot. He rose up from his crouching position over the bed and staggered backwards. I fired all the other cartridges and fell back on the pillow.

"I saw him fall. I did not know much else that happened except I heard my children crying, and I knew I would not have any more trouble."

Not from him. But trouble lay ahead.

3. The Arrest

CHAUFFEUR DRIVES WOMAN TO JAIL

Thursday, 7/12/1916 (*New York Herald*). The shots were heard by John Cummings, the chauffeur, who occupied a room on the ground floor, and by Eugene Graaf, the gardener, and his wife, the housekeeper.

Cummings was the first to enter the bedroom. He had heard two other quarrels the same night and had not slept much. He saw Beutinger's body lying near a window, with the children about it, and Mrs. Beutinger said to him, "Here, John, is the pistol. Take it away. I've finished him at last, and he won't cause any more trouble. You had better telephone for Chief Harkey and tell him all about it, as I am tired."

The chief and Dr. George E. Verbeck, the family physician, arrived at the same time. To them Mrs. Beutinger said:

"I had to finish him. He tried to kill me. I shot him to save myself."

She had remained in bed until then but became partly hysterical, and the physician quieted her with a sedative before she could go on and tell of the years of indignities she had suffered.

When her housekeeper had attired her and after she had a cup of coffee, County Recorder William H. McChesney was called to the house, and he held court in the drawing room. He committed Mrs. Beutinger to the County Jail on a charge of murder, explaining that he could do nothing else. Her attorney, Walter Brandley, arrived.

County officials were called, and later in the day she became calm enough to be arraigned in the county prosecutor's office and then removed to the jail in Newark.

Before being driven to the jail in her own automobile by her own chauffeur, Mrs. Beutinger arranged with neighbors to take care of her children. The servants were left in charge of the house, and Beutinger's body was sent to a morgue in Orange.

KILLER COLLAPSES

Wednesday, 7/12/1916 (*New York Evening World*). Mrs. Beutinger collapsed in the Essex County Jail in Newark and passed from one fainting spell to another. She was attended by Dr. Edward W. Markens, who said she was suffering from hysteria.

Just what a male doctor would say. That word, hysteria,

or a version of it, is used by these (presumably) male newspaper writers seven times in this book; I counted. It stems from the Greek word "hystera," meaning "uterus" and was a shorthand way to dismiss the understandable anguish expressed by a woman who had just killed her husband.

Jailed, Mrs. B. was visited by an attorney named Frank C. McDermott, to whom she wrote a check for five hundred dollars as a retainer. He helped draft a statement under her name and read it out to a small crowd of journalists and others.

"My husband was pronounced a prince among men, but he was a devil to his family. No matter what they do to me, I can't be any worse off than living with him. It was a question of his life or mine. I did it for the sake of my children."

Mrs. Beutinger has little hope of freedom. She spent ninety minutes with another of her lawyers, Walter Brandley, who announced that the case would have to run its course. She is held on an unbailable charge — murder.

She is eager to see her children, but they cannot visit the jail and are being cared for by servants at home in Caldwell.

The children were crying when their mother was taken to Newark, but today they seemed more cheerful at home.

"My mama has gone away, but she'll be back today," little Marie said. "My papa is dead and gone to heaven. Mama killed him; that's why she went away. We were all asleep, but we woke because there was a lot of noise, and we heard Mama scream. Papa and Mama had been mad at each other."

In the Spanish War Beutinger was a private in the U.S. Army. Later he became a sergeant and was attached to the Quartermaster's Department in the Philippines until two years ago.

About two years ago they lived in New Rochelle at 308 Clinton Place and, according to their neighbors, they quarreled continually. Their children went to the Sinclair School, near Hastings. Mrs. Beutinger obtained a separation and went to live with gardener Cummings's family at 241 South Broadway, Yonkers.

One can only imagine the fuss at the Essex County Jail when the aristocratic Mrs. Beutinger was booked in and lodged there with the other women inmates — maybe a prostitute or two, maybe a teenage runaway, maybe a puzzled old woman who had been caught with a package of macaroni as she tried to leave a market without paying for it.

I can picture Margaret Beutinger sleeping off a doctor's injection of a calming drug and then the next day, feeling a little better, pleading to see her children. Her attorney, Walter Brandley, made a few phone calls. Then the two older girls were driven the nine miles from Caldwell to Orange, and they were brought into the jail.

AND HER FIVE LITTLE KIDS ALL DRESSED IN WHITE

'PAPA HIT MY MAMA LOTS'

Thursday, 7/13/1916 (*New York Tribune*). Two little girls with bobbed brown hair and short white skirts hurried down the corridors of the Essex County Jail yesterday afternoon. The round, childish eyes of Margaret, not quite 9 years old, and Marie, 6, had seen a good deal of the cruelty visited upon their mother by their father, and had also seen him die.

Gleeful at the novelty of their excursion, they smiled at the jail officials and chattered with youthful exuberance.

"Where's Mama?" Marie asked. "Why doesn't she come to meet us?"

A door opened, and they were led into a cell. Margaret Claire Beutinger hurried forward to embrace the girls and kiss them. She sobbed.

Her chief counsel, Walter Brandley; the jail matron, and the keeper all turned away.

"Don't cry, Mama," said Marie as she put up a little brown hand to pat her mother's cheek.

"They brought us candy, and we put it on the top shelf, and we aren't going to eat it till you come home," Margaret offered, by way of supreme consolation.

Later, at home in Caldwell, Margaret told her story to a reporter as casually as if she were reciting the events at a doll's tea party.

"I didn't like my papa as much as my mama," she said. "When he got mad, he pounded the table with my dolls, even my best one, and never thought of how Dolly would feel. My mama wouldn't do a thing like that.

"He swore at Freddy and me when we said our prayers the way the Sisters taught us. Then he hit Mama when she asked him not to let us hear him swear.

"He hit her lots of times. She would cry, and then we would cry, too. Last week he hurt her eye so much it is all black yet. Have you seen my pretty mama?

"I woke up when the shot went off. Mama was standing by her bed, right next to ours, in her nightgown, and I heard her scream. I didn't know what the matter was, but I thought my papa had hit her again. Papa was sitting in the rocking chair by the window, and he said, 'I'll kill you yet,' and I was scared. But Mama said, 'No, you won't bother me any more.'"

This is a nice recounting, but Marie is telling it differently from her mother, at least the way the reporter gives it. And that was exactly what later troubled a jury as well: Who was to know exactly what happened? What witnesses to believe? It would be the jury's tough job to do exactly that.

"Billy see it, too," chuckled the three-year-old baby, evidently regarding the entire account as a story told for his amusement. He climbed onto the reporter's lap and then slid down again.

"I like my mama better'n you," he said. "I ain't your boy."

4. The Funeral

WIFE DIRECTS DETAILS

Thursday, 7/13/1916 (*New York Evening World*). Mrs. Beutinger, bitterly disappointed that she would not be allowed to attend the funeral of her husband this afternoon in the family home, nevertheless has been active in arranging the details.

Captain Calvin A. Lenthold, connected with the headquarters of the Army's Department of the East at Governor's Island, a friend of the dead man, called at the jail last night and offered to take charge of the funeral. Mrs. Beutinger thanked him but said she preferred to look after the arrangements herself.

Early this morning, at her request, her lawyer asked acting prosecutor Mott to permit her presence at the rites under the guard of deputy sheriffs. After a lengthy conference, the request was denied because there was no precedent for such action.

"Although I can't go myself," she sobbed, "I want to

see that my children pay proper respect to the memory of their father."

The estimates of Beutinger's wealth were declared today to be greatly exaggerated. Acquaintances said he was worth less than $20,000.

NO TEARS SHED

Friday, 7/14/1916 (*New York Tribune*). Not one tear was shed at the funeral service for Christof Beutinger yesterday afternoon in the family home on Hillcrest Road in Caldwell, New Jersey.

And nowhere in the prayers or the readings was any mention made of the man who lay dead.

Five little children, their eyes bright with curiosity, were lifted one by one to the level of the coffin to look upon the face of their father, a bullet wound in his forehead.

In the big, silent room with its funeral wreaths and its weight of gloom, the five looked small and pitiable, little homesick aliens in an unknown country of sorrow and tragedy.

"Thou hast set our iniquities before us," intoned the solemn voice of the minister. "Who knoweth the power of Thine anger?"

Mrs. Beutinger had insisted that her children should honor their father and that their mourning should be complete, even to the tiny, black-bordered handkerchiefs they carried.

"He was their father," she said earlier. "Some day my babies may judge me for my action in ending an unendurable horror. Even from them I want no more sympathy than is fair. Let them go to the funeral and remember their father as kindly as they can."

So the frightened little procession came into a room that was almost empty. Had it not been for the children, the father would have gone almost unattended to the grave. Beside them were only the minister, the defense lawyer, the housekeeper, the gardener, and two men and two women who had come from New York and who declined to give their names.

The services were simple. Not once did the Reverend John E. Klein, pastor of the German Evangelical Church of Orange, mention the name of the dead man. Instead, he prayed:

"Be with these little children who have been afflicted. If it be Thy will, restore their mother to them soon."

The room, darkened by a thunderstorm outside, was from time to time brightened by flashes of lightning as the children stood about the coffin. Three-year-old Billy, the baby, hid his frightened face in the neck of Mrs. Eugene Graaf, the housekeeper. Then he lifted it and asked about his father:

"What's he doing?"

"Hush, darling, he's asleep," was the response.

As she carried the child from the room, the boy looked back over her shoulder, puzzled. The other children were quiet and made no display.

Outside, curious busybodies stood in the rain to watch the casket carried to a hearse. They buzzed over the details of the crime and did not disperse until the last car of the cortege was out of sight.

The interment was in Prospect Hill Cemetery, barely half a mile from the Beutinger home *(photo adjacent)*. The five children stood in the rain while the casket was lowered. Billy, perhaps frightened for the first time, slipped his hand into that of Walter Brandley, his mother's attorney, and 8-year-old Margaret stopped to straighten one of the wreaths.

The little party lingered about the grave only long enough to hear the minister's "Dust to dust, ashes to ashes," then turned briskly away.

"I am glad it is over," Mrs. Beutinger said in her cell last night. "I wanted to go myself, but I am glad the children were there."

Attorney Brandley has told the defendant that there could be nothing done to hasten the legal process, and it is probable she will have to remain locked up until the grand jury meets in the fall.

5. Summer 1916

SYMPATHY FOR ACCUSED WOMAN

Thursday, 7/13/1916 (*New York Evening World*). The widespread sympathy for Mrs. Beutinger is evidenced by the report from her attorney, Frank McDermott of Newark, New Jersey, that many people, mostly strangers, have offered to post bail for her, up to a million dollars if necessary.

McDermott announced that John F. Brennan, a Yonkers lawyer who is familiar with Mrs. Beutinger's affairs, will be associated with him in the preparation of the case. They will claim she acted in self-defense and that she was temporarily unbalanced at the time.

They actually did not use the latter argument, only the former, self-defense — much stronger, in my opinion.

Mrs. Beutinger says she has no regrets and believes her

husband was insane as a result of the climate in the Philippines, where they had lived.

Not very likely, or you would have millions of crazy Filipinos.

EX-ATTORNEY-GENERAL IS HIRED

Sunday, 7/16/1916 (*Trenton Evening Times*). Robert H. McCarter, former attorney-general and one of the ablest lawyers in the State *(pictured)*, has been retained to defend Mrs. Beutinger, he said at his summer home in Rumson.

He had a talk with her and took her statement.

Frank M. McDermott, who claimed to have been retained by the woman early this week, has no connection with the case.

MRS. BEUTINGER CHEERFUL

Friday, 7/16/1916 (*New York Sun*). Walter Brandley, her counsel, along with Robert H. McCarter, will endeavor to show she killed her husband in self-defense.

She eats and sleeps well and keeps her spirits cheerful despite the realization that she will have to spend the rest of the summer in jail.

STATE WILL OPPOSE BAIL

Friday, 7/21/1916 (*New York Tribune*). Assistant county prosecutor Andrew Van Blarcom will oppose any move to admit Mrs. Beutinger to bail. He will argue that the inmate cannot allege self-defense because New Jersey law holds that before firing in one's own defense one must make every effort to escape from the assailant.

He will seek to show that her killing of her husband was premeditated.

ABUSED WIFE WAS ASHAMED

Saturday, 7/22/1916 (*Kingston Gleaner*). Dr. E. I. Ives of Little Falls, New Jersey, has confirmed that Mrs. Beutinger had suffered abuse at the hands of her wealthy husband.

Not wishing the neighbors to know of her humiliation, Mrs. Beutinger asked her housekeeper to obtain a physician who did not live in Caldwell, and Mrs. Graaf called Dr. Ives.

"I found that she had been severely beaten, and I attended her for many bruises and abrasions," he said.

"After that, she called at my office almost every week,

AND HER FIVE LITTLE KIDS ALL DRESSED IN WHITE

KILLED HER WEALTHY HUSBAND

(Photo by A. Duperly and Son)

Mrs. M. C. Beutinger Says She was Attacked Before She Fired

LADY WHO IS WELL-KNOWN IN JAMAICA.

Divorced Her Husband Some Time Ago & Came To Parents Here.

COUPLE THEN RE-MARRIED.

Held now on Charge of Murder; Says She Endured Indignities.

HOW THE TRAGEDY OCCURRED

In yesterday's Gleaner we published a report of a tragedy at Caldwell, New Jersey, U. S. A., when Mrs. Margaret Claire Beutinger is alleged to have shot and killed her husband at their residence on the morning of the 11th instant.

Mrs. Beutinger is a Jamaican, a daughter of Mr. George Abrahams of "Arlington", St. Andrew, and is well known here.

She has several sisters, some of whom are married.

The "New York Herald" of July 12th, published the following account of the tragedy:

"Christopher Beutinger, wealthy coal commission merchant, with offices at No. 1 Broadway and formerly United States purchasing agent in the Philippines, was shot and killed yesterday by his young wife, Mrs. Margaret Claire Beutinger, in the bedroom of their country residence at Caldwell, N. J.

When pressed to reveal causes that led to the tragedy, Mrs. Beutinger said last night:—

"Secondarily, he was an ardent German and perhaps I never could forget that I am an Englishwoman. In the nine years we were married, I bore him seven children, five of

MRS. MARGARET CLAIRE BEUTINGER.

often with new cuts and scratches, saying her husband had done it. Once she told me she knew her husband was going to kill her some day, and once she said she believed him insane, that the war had caused him to lose his mind."

Interesting how she blamed the climate and then the Spanish-American War for her husband's character. She didn't blame him as a person; they had had many good times together, and she was seizing on any reason at all to explain his errant behavior. Next she blamed the Great War then raging in Europe and around the world.

Mrs. Graaf and the other household help told attorney Brandley that Beutinger was such an ardent German sympathizer that his mind had been turned. He frequently prefaced his blows with "You Englishwoman!" or "You're English!"

Margaret Beutinger was brought before a judge to see if there was enough evidence to hold her. Not just any judge, but the chief justice of New Jersey.

STORY CALLED INCONSISTENT

Tuesday, 7/25/1916 (*New York Tribune*). At a preliminary hearing, Chief Justice William B. Gummere declared yesterday that while he sympathized as a man with Mrs. Beutinger, as a Justice of the Supreme Court he had to deny her request for bail.

Mrs. Beutinger's attorney, Robert H. McCarter, offered any amount of bond and pleaded that the woman's physical condition, coupled with the fact that she was about to become a mother again and that her five children needed her, entitled her to bail.

I left "about to become a mother" in the above excerpt to illustrate how two reporters can hear the same words and get something entirely different from them. A different writer, for the New York Evening World, had it as "the woman's physical condition" and nothing about motherhood. Of course, Mrs. B. may not have been pregnant at all, despite what the Tribune reported — and never followed up.

But Gummere replied that the woman's story, as presented in a lengthy affidavit, showed inconsistencies.

For example, she had failed to explain fully how fear had caused her to arm herself. She had not made clear what happened in the first and second trips of her husband to her room. She had not told all that occurred during the final visit, when she pulled the trigger five times.

An affidavit by Sergeant Walter Godfrey of the prosecutor's office was a point against the woman's story. The sergeant thought that Mrs. Beutinger could have escaped since she was nearer the door than her husband.

This doesn't make a lot of sense. If she had run out the door, Christof could have followed her out. And probably would have — with consequences to her. Still, Gummere was following the law as he saw it.

The chief justice said:

"If I were charging a grand jury, I would have to say, 'Gentlemen, with these facts before you it is your duty to indict this woman for murder and leave it to the trial jury after they have heard her story to decide her innocence or her guilt.'"

WHY DID SHE STICK AROUND?

Monday, 7/24/1916 (*New York Evening World*). Chief Justice Gummere said Mrs. Beutinger's story was sprinkled with inconsistencies. It was hard for him to understand why she remarried a man she had divorced and whom she had said a dog could not trust.

The justice remarked that Mrs. Beutinger must have known that her husband's nature and habits would not change during the time they lived apart.

Gummere bound Mrs. B over for trial in the next session of the court in the fall.

It's pretty obvious this man never had his consciousness raised, but what do you expect from somebody who graduated from Princeton University in 1870? (Princeton did not admit women as students until — wait for it! — 1969.)

Because of Justice Gummere's antediluvian views, Mrs. B. had to make the Essex County Jail her home for three more months.

6. The First Trial

Court was called to order on Tuesday morning, October 23, 1916, in the Essex County courthouse (postcard pictured), and the five Beutinger children were in the massive, ornate chamber, as they were to be almost every day until the end of their mother's travail some two months later.

Public prosecutor Jacob L. Newman commented that he didn't believe it was proper for the kids to be in the spectators' gallery. He was prescient, for the children turned out to be the center of everybody's attention — including the jury's. And the newspaper reporters'.

ON TRIAL FOR MURDER

Wednesday, 10/25/1916 (*New York Evening World*). The trial moved rapidly today in Newark, the first witness being called just an hour after Judge William F. Martin assumed the bench.

Mrs. Beutinger sat with her white-gloved hands in her lap, more like a spectator than a defendant on trial for her life.

Three little daughters and two little sons were seated among the spectators behind her. They bobbed their heads about to peep between the shoulders of those in front.

Mrs. Beutinger is a slender, diminutive woman who appeared even more so today as she sat beside Florence Hall, the court matron, a sturdy woman of evident strength, wearing handcuffs like a charm bracelet.

The defendant's first tears came when Robert H. McCarter, her counsel, told the jury of the treatment her husband had subjected her to. He pointed to her as a delicate little woman, only five feet tall, while Beutinger was a burly six-footer who weighed more than two hundred pounds.

On the wall in back of the witness chair was mounted a large floor plan of the $25,000 Beutinger home, with the bedroom where Beutinger was killed conspicuously outlined. *(Homes in that area are going for about half a million dollars today.)*

Within two minutes after 10 o'clock, the drawing of the jury began. By 11 o'clock it was chosen.

The jury members, all men of course, as was the custom of that day, were:

From Norwalk, Leo A. Baum, manufacturing jeweler, foreman; Joseph Budd, insurance man; Edson L. Clark, mercantile manager; Emil Haesner, secretary; F.J. McLaughlin, collector; Frank Williams, banker; Alfred L. Cooper, accountant, and William Gosberg, insurance man; from East Orange, Raymond J. Freeman, manager, and Charles A. Christian, retired; and from Irvington, William R. Clark, salesman, and William J. Mayer, clerk.

COURT HASTENS PROCEEDINGS

Thursday, 10/26/1916 (*The New York Times*). The case was conducted with such expedition yesterday that by the middle of the afternoon the prosecution had presented all its witnesses, including Mrs. Beutinger's housekeeper and chauffeur.

The only defense witness was John S. Provost, who testified to the accuracy of a diagram of the house that he had drawn.

CHILDREN LOOK ON AS TRIAL BEGINS

Thursday, 10/26/1916 (*New York Tribune*). Mrs. Beutinger has begun her fight for freedom, making self-defense her plea.

THE BATTERED WIFE

She is not fighting alone. Two rows behind her as she faced the judge was her strongest reinforcing army. Her five little children, round-faced and babyish, in their white sailor suits or crisp white frocks, sat swinging their short legs all day long, while they listened without comprehension to the story of their father's brutality and their mother's crime.

AND HER FIVE LITTLE KIDS ALL DRESSED IN WHITE

The defense team was waging much of its battle in the Court of Public Opinion. It was no coincidence that newspapers around the country, and in Hawaii and in the West Indies, were filled with photographs of the battered wife and her five little kids all dressed in white.

It was a public-relations campaign of the first stripe, waged by a very experienced defense team that had not been idle in preparing the case during Mrs. B's summer-long incarceration. These are new clothes you see in the photo, which I bet was taken when the children were allowed to visit her in the Essex County lockup. This winsome photo was widely printed in many newspapers throughout the country.

The five were the chief figures of interest yesterday in the crowded courtroom, where assistant county prosecutor Wilbur A. Mott will try to prove that Mrs. Beutinger's act was premeditated murder and must be punished as such.

Men about to be sworn as jurors looked at the row of little white figures and asked to be excused from serving. Mrs. Beutinger's attorney, Robert H. McCarter, the witnesses on the stand, and even the lawyers for the prosecution glanced at the children and lowered their voices as they recounted the details of the tragedy.

That lawyer McCarter was a sly fox, wasn't he, to have the kids all dressed in white? Not to mention Mrs. Beutinger's gloves.

With her white-gloved hands folded calmly in her lap,

and the curve of her cheek hidden by her white fox fur, the 27-year-old defendant listened impassively to the evidence.

She was the only woman in the courtroom who did not shudder when the prosecution introduced into evidence the five bullets that figured in the tragedy or when a witness described details of the autopsy and the course of the bullets through Beutinger's body.

Only twice in the day did the tired mask of mere polite interest drop from her pretty face.

As she was escorted into the court in the custody of Mrs. Florence Bell of the sheriff's office and took her seat, daughter Margaret asked in a shrill whisper, "Why don't Mama sit here with us?" A flash of pain crossed Mrs. Beutinger's face, and she turned quickly to smile at the children as they sat with her sister, Mrs. Jennie Herron, who had come from the West Indies to be at the trial.

Later, Billy, bored by the slow course of the law, began to cry, and his mother pursed her lips reprovingly as if to say, "Naughty!"

During the course of the defense argument, lawyer McCarter told the jury that Mrs. Beutinger had returned to her husband after divorcing him for her children's sake and upon the plea of the Mother Superior of the convent in which she had placed them.

He quoted, "A woman, a dog, and a chestnut tree. The more you beat them, the better they be" in explaining Mrs. Beutinger's long suffering in her marriage.

Now that doesn't make a lick of sense to me, but I'm sure

this lawyer, the state's former attorney-general, intended this doggerel verse to have some kind of weird positive effect on the all-male jury.

• • •

Newspapers were assigning women reporters to cover the trial. The New York Evening World sent Nixola Greeley-Smith, its famous "sob sister," as these newswomen were sometimes dismissively called, to the Newark courthouse.

In the image from the New York Evening World, next page, Judge William F. Martin is at the left, and defense counsel Robert H. McCarter is standing at a large drawing of the Beutinger house, with a pointer. Assistant prosecutor Wilbur A. Mott is seated near him. Matron Florence Bell and Mrs. Beutinger are in the center, and the children are with their aunt, Jennie Herron.

IS A WOMAN OWNER OF HER OWN SOUL?
By Nixola Greeley-Smith

Thursday, 10/26/1916 (*New York Evening World*). Five little children sat solemnly on a bench in the Essex County Courthouse in Newark, as if in school.

Before them was mounted a huge blackboard with a map on it — a murder map on which the prosecutor was undertaking to prove that their mother, Margaret Claire Beutinger, murdered their father, Christof, in the early morning hours of July 11.

THE BATTERED WIFE

The map bored the children. Their eyes followed the long wand that the prosecutor used to indicate Room A and Hall B and "Mr. Beutinger's bedroom, E," wandered to their little, mouselike mother for a moment, and then gradually blurred into sleep. Murder demonstrated like a proposition in geometry was of no interest to them.

Billy, a sailor boy all in white, slept peacefully, except for one moment when he awoke to the glittering reflection of an object in the hand of assistant prosecutor Wilbur A. Mott — the revolver from which his mother fired five shots into the body of his father.

A modern principle as well as a woman are both on trial in that arched and frescoed courtroom of Essex County

— whether a woman is the owner of her own body. A few hundred years ago, when women were bartered like sheep or goats, this principle would have been laughed at.

Today it is being tested at a murder trial.

Mrs. Beutinger wore a pair of spotless, new white gloves. Her shepherd's plaid suit hung on the figure of a little girl. Her small, round hat, a black sailor, was draped with a veil of black lace *(nice touch!)*, and a stole of white fox wound her slender throat, softening the tension of her tight little jaws.

That tension increased when Eugene Graaf, her chauffeur, testified she told him that she had warned Beutinger, "I'll finish you!" and her husband had responded, heatedly, "Go ahead and do it, then!"

Otherwise, Graaf's story was the same as the gardener's, John Cummings's, that he had entered the room to find Beutinger's body on the floor and Mrs. Beutinger on the bed sobbing, while 9-year-old Margaret was bent over trying to comfort her.

Mrs. Beutinger shot her husband after he had forced an entrance into the room she occupied with her two little girls, Margaret and Marie. She shot him after a struggle when she realized that her stratagem of using her little children as a protection against her husband had not availed and, she says, after Beutinger had threatened her life if she continued to resist him.

The Beutingers had quarreled for years, and the wife had divorced him for his cruelty and abuse only to remarry him a few months later so that her children "would not grow up like little heathens."

THE BATTERED WIFE

Mrs. Beutinger returned to her home from a hospital the first week of July. Before then, the couple had slept in the same room. The housekeeper, Mrs. Graaf, testified that Beutinger had occupied Room F, away from his wife, since July 5. *(That would be five nights of sleeping apart.)*

It was a room with two beds, and the two little Beutinger girls were sleeping in their father's bed when, clad in a dressing gown and night robe, he stole upon their mother in the gray dawn. Twice she ordered him out. When he returned a third time and threatened her life, she shot him.

A few minutes later the housekeeper, roused by the shots, came in and heard her say, "He won't bother me any more."

The shame and terror of that hour when she wavered between desperate aversion and a mother's desire to protect the innocence of her sleeping children is still written upon her face. The nose is arched and high, the mouth a mere pucker. Because of the narrowness of her face, Mrs. Beutinger's profile suggests a cut-paper silhouette. It is expressionless save for the shadowed, smoldering, dark eyes.

Yesterday she smiled or laughed all through the testimony of her gardener-chauffeur, John Cummings, a rather green Irish lad, and she sobbed bitterly during the summation of her counsel, Robert H. McCarter, to the jury.

The impression one gets from the little woman's face is a mouselike timidity. She may have been unnecessarily afraid of her husband. As a man said yesterday in the court, "How much simpler to lock the key in her bedroom door than to wait for him to come back and then kill him!"

But nearly all deeds of violence are the result of fear, and even great heroes have explained their valor by saying simply that they were afraid to run away.

Billy slept in the arms of his aunt, Mrs. Herron, whose vivid, robust beauty made the little courtroom look as if some great, red cactus were abloom in it. It may be that little Mrs. Beutinger herself looked like a tropical flower before the years of violence and abuse began.

GARDENER RAISES A LAUGH

Friday, 10/27/1916 (*New York Sun*). NEWARK, October 26 — Young Cummings proved a valuable witness for the defense on Wednesday. In a quaint Irish brogue he told of the beatings and verbal abuse he had seen and heard his employer bestow on Mrs. Beutinger.

"Mr. Beutinger said to me, 'What a temper my wife has got,' and I said to him, 'Mr. Beutinger, if she was an Irish woman she'd break every chair in the house.'"

That raised a laugh from the spectators which brought a quick rebuke from the judge.

Mrs. Beutinger was put on the stand to tell her story. Each journalist — and there were many in the courtroom — wrote up exactly the same circumstance each in his or her own way, as you can tell by many of these articles. Sometimes readers would buy two or three papers so they could get the full thrust of the day's events.

Which was — Mrs. B was sleeping away from her husband, in a suite with two bedrooms and one bathroom. The three boys were in a far bedroom. Little Margaret and Marie were in one bed in the same room as their mother, who occupied the other bed. Mrs. B had a pistol in the room. She had put five bullets in the chambers.

Her husband barged in three times during the night. And here's where the narrative becomes tenuous. What did he want? Simply to berate his wife — to beat her up — or to rape her? The newspaper reports, in the custom of the day, never delved far into the realm of sex ("Children might read this"). The word "attack" was often a substitute for the word "rape."

Claire Beutinger testified that her husband knelt on her chest and threatened to beat her if she "repulsed him." Every newspaper reader thought the worst of Christof Beutinger's motives when he forced his way into his wife's room three times in one night, and they did not need it spelled out in four-letter words to understand.

SOBBING MRS. BEUTINGER'S EVIDENCE

Thursday, 10/26/1916 (*New York Herald*). Mrs. Beutinger told of her marriage, a short residence in New York, and then a move to the Philippines, where her husband was a clerk in the quartermaster's office.

Even then, in her first married year, Christof struck and abused her, she said. He took to drinking and gambling and lost large sums of money. When she complained, he beat her worse than ever. He kicked her at times when her physical condition was delicate.

"But you loved him?" she was asked.

"Yes, there never was a time when I did not love him," she replied.

Asked about the morning of her husband's death, Mrs. Beutinger testified:

"I was still weak and ill from the beatings he had given me during the previous week," she said. "My husband came into my room three times. My little girls — Margaret and Marie — were sleeping in the same room.

"Twice I drove him out. Then I put a revolver I had just purchased under the bedclothes. He came in again.

"'Chris,' I said. 'I am through with you. I am going to divorce you.'

"His eyes were bulging. He was cursing me and making toward my bed as if to carry out his threat of strangling me. I was sick, weak, terrorized by his brutality and still sore and scarcely able to see because of the beatings he had given me. My left eye was black and blue, and closed.

"I was frantic. And so I took the revolver that I had placed in bed with me, and as I screamed in fright, my finger contracted on the trigger. I screamed — and screamed — and the shots sounded out, one after the other, as my hand tightened on the handle of the weapon.

"He staggered back and then fell, and I kept on screaming and pulling the trigger until only empty clicks sounded and the pistol wouldn't work any more."

THE BATTERED WIFE

Her voice was high-pitched and quavering from sobs. Her little shoulders were shaking.

Her attorney asked:

"And then, when the pistol wouldn't work any more and only clicks came from it, your husband was dead?"

"Yes," she replied, her head bowed. "He was dead."

There was a long silence in the courtroom, and some furtive use of handkerchiefs by dozens of the spectators — men as well as women — and some jurors, too. It was, really, as tragic a moment as any one there cared to pass through.

The little woman on the stand was almost broken. Facing her from the first row of spectators' seats were her five small children.

There is no question as to her technical guilt. It remains merely for the jury to say whether she was justified in slaying the man who was "built like Jack Johnson," as she put it, who weighed two hundred fifty pounds, and who, by her tale, was a drunken brute, who even beat their little children as well as herself — and she is a tiny creature of a few more than one hundred pounds.

Johnson, the heavyweight champion of the world, pictured, weighed two hundred pounds when he was in top condition.

WIFE TELLS OF KILLING

Friday, 10/27/1916 (*The New York Times*). First calmly and then in a voice shaken by sobs, Mrs. Beutinger told how she shot and killed her husband because he had attacked her twice before in the night and she feared he meant, on his third visit, to injure her badly, perhaps to kill her.

She prefaced her story with a detailed account of their married life, which was made unbearable by frequent attacks, insults, and brutalities.

She told of their marriage in Kingston, Jamaica, in 1906, after they met on a voyage from New York. They traveled through the United States, Europe, Siberia, Shanghai, the Philippines, and Honolulu.

Her husband consistently drank to excess and was cruel to her, sometimes threatening to kill her, until she divorced him last year, put the children in a convent, and went to live in Mount Vernon under an assumed name — only to yield to his entreaty for a new chance; they remarried on December 29.

The beatings and chokings continued, as did her husband's heavy drinking, and after a scene in which he struck one of his daughters and tried to gouge out his wife's eyes, she said she was through and would never be a wife to him again. That day she got a revolver.

On the night of July 10 he forced his way into her room twice, knelt on her chest and threatened to kill her if she repulsed him, and it was on his third visit that she told him she was going to get a divorce again.

"Then he rushed toward me with his right hand upraised and a glazed look in his bulging eyes," she said. "I screamed and screamed as he came on, and I reached under the pillow for my revolver. He rushed toward me, and I shot.

"Marie and Margaret crept from their bed in the room and clung to me. I got out of my bed with the revolver pointed away so I should not hurt them accidentally. Then I sank back. Little Marie got a wet towel and bathed my head, and then the servants came."

Mrs. Beutinger said there had been insanity in her husband's family, a brother having died of it in 1914.

SHE JUST LOST CONTROL

Friday, 10/27/1916 (*New York Tribune*). In a kind of dull wail, but with no display of emotion, she told her story of ten years of brutality and abasement, beginning with her honeymoon and not ceasing until she stopped the terror with five revolver shots.

"I was always afraid," was her summary.

Her tale was impressive in its simplicity. Two nights previous he had taken a doll from Margaret, the oldest child. The child sobbed and the mother protested; he blackened his wife's eye and tried to choke her, then turned his attention to the child.

"I said, 'Don't do that. You can strike me, but you can't strike the children.'"

On the night of the killing, he came into the bedroom where his wife lay and swore that he would kill her.

"I told him I would protect myself and that I meant business. 'You do?' he said. He was coming toward me. Dr. Curtis had given me something to put on my eye, and I couldn't see much out of it. I could just see his hand coming toward my throat, and then I saw his eyes bulging.

"He came toward me quickly. I screamed, and all the shots went off as I screamed for help. I couldn't stop firing. I had lost control of my muscles. Then I don't remember anything, except Margaret pulling me toward the bed and little Marie holding a wet towel to my face. And he was dead."

WRENCHING TESTIMONY IN NEWARK

Friday, 10/27/1916 (*New York Sun*). Stark, startling realism of the most sickening type wrote itself into the Essex court records yesterday.

In most trials, however dreadful the circumstances, there is some relief; there are a few highlights of humor, but there was nothing but sordid ugliness in the tale of suffering and persecution that Margaret Claire Beutinger told in half-faltering, half-hysterical tones.

The impassiveness she had maintained was gone. Her delicately cut features were stained with tears. Sometimes when her lawyer pressed her for details of her husband's abuse — horrible and unprintable some of them — her voice grew inaudible and her fingers picked at her black-bordered handkerchief. Then she would raise it to her nose and blow a good, honest blast that showed how real her crying was, and her words would come with a sobbing rush, like a child trying to get the tale of its wrongs out all at once.

Through the hours of her testimony and cross-examination, she never once looked at her children, who sat in a row, five tiny brunette copies of their mother, well up at the front of the chamber.

Six other witnesses testified afterward: John Cummings, the chauffeur who took the pistol from her after the shooting, his second time on the stand; Mrs. Julia Cummings, his aunt, with whom Mrs. Beutinger and the children had taken refuge in Yonkers after her divorce; Police Chief Harkey of Caldwell; Dr. George V. Verbeck, Dr. Edwin Ives, and Dr. Herbert Simmons, all of whom in different ways corroborated Mrs. Beutinger's tale of violence and diabolical pursuit.

It has been a disputed point as to how much religion had to do with Mrs. Beutinger's remarriage in December 1915. The judge, however, shot down an attempt to place this topic into evidence when the defense put a lawyer, Frances H. Donahue, on the stand. She had consulted him for advice.

"You advised a reconciliation?" attorney McCarter asked the other lawyer.

"I did," he replied.

"Are you a Catholic?" demanded McCarter.

Assistant prosecutor Mott jumped up with an objection, and Judge Martin said he did not see what the question had to do with the case.

"Your honor," McCarter explained, "my opponent has asked with a sneer why this woman went back to the man from whom she had fled. I propose to prove by the witness that Mrs. Beutinger, who is a Catholic, was persuaded by him, by her priest, and by the Mother Superior of the convent in which she had placed her children that it was her duty to return to her husband."

"Ruled out," said the judge, and the witness was excused.

At one point, Mrs. Beutinger's testimony threatened to undo her attorney's strategy of pleading self-defense.

First, she described a quarrel at the supper table on July 5.

"I had bought Margaret and Marie a doll," she said. "He asked me whose money I had used, and I said mine. He called me a liar and a ..." She hesitated, until, questioned by her lawyer, she brought out an epithet that has not been used since the time of King John.

Then he began twisting the doll's legs, Margaret cried, and he struck the child.

In a quavering voice, she told of more abuse, which led her to send for the pistol. On the following Sunday, her husband came to the room where she had locked herself in, but it wasn't until Monday night that the tragedy unfolded.

"He began quarreling with me while the boys were saying their prayers, I went to bed, and soon he forced his way into my room.

"I said, 'Chris, I can't have any more to do with you; I can't be your wife,' but he seized me and pulled me out of bed, and then I got to the bureau where the pistol was and snatched it out. His eyes bulged out, he lashed at me, fast, fast, with his hands" — and here the little woman raised her own hands and shook them, her voice rising to a shriek — "and he cried 'I'll get you!' and then I screamed, and shot, and I screamed and screamed, and every time I screamed the pistol went off."

On cross-examination, the prosecutor asked, "What was in your thought when you shot? Were you in fear for your life, or was the shooting accidental?"

"Both," she said, almost in a whisper.

This article differed from the others, which reported that the pistol was drawn from beneath a pillow.

It was a wandering life that Beutinger led his wife during the ten years she lived with him, but whether they were in the Philippines, where he served the government — and grafted from it, according to her — or the West Indies, in Germany, or the United States, he was equally energetic in abusing her. In that decade she bore him seven children, two of whom died.

Much of the time they lived on money provided by her father.

The gambling and grafting brought tension between them, and sometimes she would threaten to report him, and he would rage at her. Once, however, she did make an unsuccessful journey to Washington to intercede with the Secretary of War on his behalf. He therefore "got a chance to resign" before he was fired, she said.

"Why did you threaten your husband that you would report him?" asked prosecutor Mott.

"I wanted him to try to be good. I was always trying to get him to stop gambling and grafting."

The feeling in the courtroom is that tomorrow the defense will rest, the lawyers will sum up, the jury will make a decision, and Mrs. Beutinger will go home a free woman.

'A MOST BRUTAL MAN'

Thursday, 10/26/1916 (*Bridgeton, New Jersey, Evening News*, by United Press wire). Blushing deeply and with eyes downcast, Mrs. Margaret Beutinger told in dramatic fashion why she shot and killed her husband.

"He was a most brutal man," she testified. "From the time I married him until the time I shot him he constantly made demands on me which were impossible to fulfill.

"When I refrained, he threatened to kill me. He was physically built like a Jack Johnson, huge physically, and of course I was afraid of him.

"He beat me in Washington, and then we went to Philadelphia and Chicago. While in Chicago he made me get out of bed one night because of my physical condition."

The women in the courtroom knew what "physical condi-

tion" meant. Seldom did anybody hear or use the word "menstruation" in public. But even if some of the lurid but exact testimony was not printed in the newspaper, the female spectators in the courtroom would make known to their women friends later on just what exactly had been said.

Dorothy Dix, the famed advice columnist whose work was syndicated all over the nation, also covered the trial, as she did many others where a woman had killed her husband or lover. When the prosecution asked Mrs. Beutinger why she had made no attempt to protect herself from her husband, Dix responded:

A CYNICAL SMILE
By Dorothy Dix

Tuesday, 10/3/1916 (*New York Journal):* Every woman will smile cynically at the naive suggestion that a wife can protect herself against her husband. We are all helpless when the enemy is one of our own household.

FINAL DEFENSE WITNESSES

Saturday, 10/28/1916 (*New York Tribune*). Witness Julia Ann Gasco was greeted yesterday with rapturous kisses thrown by the small Beutingers when they saw her in the courtroom. She had been a servant in the Beutinger household just last year: She testified that Beutinger had made advances on her and that he tried to throw her down a flight of stairs when he learned that she had told his wife. She was just 14 at the time.

Another witness, John H. De Baus, had been a passenger on a boat with the Beutingers in the Philippines. He testified that Beutinger had threatened to take his wife's life if she continued to talk about leaving him. De Baus also said that Beutinger tried to persuade him to sign a statement that he had seen a man with Mrs. Beutinger in her stateroom.

STARTLING EVIDENCE GIVEN

Friday, 10/27/1916 (*Wilkes-Barre, Pennsylvania, Times*). Christopher Beutinger, the wealthy coal broker, attempted to bring his wife into a compromising position in order to compel her to submit to his desires.

That was the testimony of defense witness John H. De Baus of Washington, D.C., as the trial neared its end today.

"Beutinger met me in Washington and wanted me to make an affidavit that I had found a man in Mrs. Beutinger's stateroom while she was nude, en route to the Philippine Islands. I told him it was impossible. He said it would help him in the future. He told me about the divorce proceedings and that if she ever tried to leave him again, he would kill her."

Anna Gasco, a 15-year-old Austrian servant girl, said Beutinger had made advances toward her while she was employed there.

Both sides rested shortly before 11 o'clock, the State offering no rebuttal witnesses.

COULD HAVE BEEN A GREAT ROMANCE

Friday, 10/27/1916 (*Wilkes-Barre, Pennsylvania, Times*). Defense attorney McCarter began his argument on Mrs. Beutinger's behalf by asserting that if it were not such a great tragedy, it might instead have been the greatest romance ever heard.

The defendant sobbed as the lawyer told of the ocean voyage of the young couple shortly after their marriage, and of their travels afterward. He pictured the change that Mrs. Beutinger found in the man with whom she had agreed to live.

She borrowed a handkerchief from the matron and buried her face in it. Her children began crying in distress.

In closing, McCarter made a stirring plea for Mrs. Beutinger's freedom.

AS BIG AS THE WORLD CHAMPION

Saturday, 10/28/1916 (*New York Tribune*). McCarter noted that the victim was "a big, masterful, handsome man weighing more than two hundred fifty pounds" and had acted as a despot from the day of the couple's marriage.

He noted that the defendant had said her husband

was the physical counterpart of Jack Johnson, but, unlike Johnson, he was only "willing to fight against women and children."

In his summation, the prosecuting attorney pleaded with the jury to convict Mrs. Beutinger despite the presence of her children in the courtroom.

'HE HAD A RIGHT TO LIVE'

Friday, 10/27/1916 (*New York Evening World*). Prosecutor Newman, addressing the jury for the State, said:

"Christof Beutinger may have been a brutal, lustful man, but he had a right to live. It is getting to be a mockery of justice that juries will not deal with a woman as they will with a man.

"This case has been well staged for sympathy, with the five little children of the defendant here in the courtroom. I want you to weigh the facts as if the defendant were not a woman, and if the facts warrant it, I ask you to convict her.

"According to her own story, she returned to live with the man who abused her. She went back to him because he was going to give her a home and an automobile.

"Let us not forget that on January 18, 1915, a preliminary decree of divorce was granted to her, and on the following May 7 the decree was made absolute, but before they were remarried on December 29, 1915, and while the divorce was pending, she lived under the same roof with

Beutinger in Yonkers. Was this the attitude of a chaste and pure woman?

"The shadow of murder was in her heart in their home in Caldwell — the tragedy of July 11 was determined upon, premeditated. Mrs. Beutinger had sent for a revolver, and in less than 24 hours, the shooting was done.

"She shot to kill; she shot five times. One bullet struck her husband in the neck; the other four bullets took a downward course, indicating that he must have been below her as he was shot — so he was either sitting or lying when the bullets were fired.

"Why did not Mrs. Beutinger lock her door against her husband? She says he made three visits. She got up between the second and third to get her revolver, and she shot him when he returned.

"There were several ways she could have escaped his advances. She could have left by another door if she did not wish to lock herself in."

Judge Martin began his charge to the jury at 2 o'clock. The room was crowded, half the spectators being women, or girls in their teens.

Martin said the jury had four choices: Conviction of first- or second-degree murder, or of manslaughter, or an acquittal.

"If the defendant had been apprehensive that her life was in danger, she had the right to protect herself, even to the point of taking the life of an adversary. The law requires that she should retreat in such a case, if she could safely do that.

"It is up to the jury to decide if she could have done so. It is also for the jury to decide whether the defendant believed herself to be in danger of her life."

The judge then took up the testimony beginning with the quarrel at dinner, over the doll, six days before the killing, up to the time the servants came into the room to find Beutinger dead on the floor.

"The State has shown that she could have escaped," the judge said. "Now, the jury has the right to consider the demeanor of the defendant on the stand and her interest in the verdict you are about to render.

"Let me call your attention to a statute passed during the last session of the Legislature. It provides that a jury may find a defendant guilty of murder in the first degree and recommend punishment by imprisonment for life."

The judge here is giving the jury the new option of finding Mrs. Beutinger guilty of murder but sparing her life, and strongly hinting it should do so.

"Sympathy, because she is a woman or on account of her children, should not sway the jury in favor of the defendant, nor against her because she deprived her five children of a father." *(This is an interesting twist.)*

CROWDS THRONG COURTHOUSE

Monday, 11/6/1916 (*Kingston Gleaner*). The general

belief was that the slender little woman would be set free within a few minutes. Almost a thousand men and women filled the corridors and stood outside the courthouse.

The Kingston Gleaner received its news from the United States days after the event.

JURY LOCKED UP FOR NIGHT

Saturday, 10/28/1916 (*The New York Times*). In Judge Martin's charge to the jury, he cautioned that, although Mrs. Beutinger's defense was that she had fired in fear of her own life, the law did not give her the right to judge for herself, but reserved such a decision to the jurors. They had to decide if she had a reasonable apprehension that her life was in danger. If so, the law allowed her to take another's life, but only if she could not retreat from the danger.

On this point, the law was explicit, the judge said: Retreat must be made if retreat were possible.

Prosecutor Newman stressed this point as well, in his summing-up.

"He went to his wife's room and demanded that she receive him. She had the right to decline. But she could have locked her bedroom door and called for help, or picked up some other weapon not so deadly as a revolver."

He said there should be no place for sympathy. And yet, he stressed:

"The stage was set for sympathy with the five little children occupying seats in the front row. The story of the defendant's unhappy life was told with tears and the gnashing of teeth. It was told to divert the minds of the jury from the evidence and to cloud their judgment.

"The fact that the defendant is a woman should make no difference."

In his turn, defense attorney Richard McCarter said:

"Gentlemen, do you wonder that this little woman raised on her arm in bed and drew that pistol? There was no retreat for her with this burly, six-foot-two, two-hundred-fifty-pound giant approaching her.

"She saw his brother already dead of insanity, and saw his upraised arm, and she began to shoot, and kept on shooting until the last chamber was emptied. What would you gentlemen have done under the circumstances?"

Jurors deliberated for 8-1/2 hours yesterday and interrupted their consideration only once, at 11 p.m. when they asked for food. After another half hour, Judge Gibson ordered they be sent to their hotel for the night and put under guard.

Friends of the defendant have begun to fear that the verdict will be against her. Some cited a recently enacted law giving trial juries the privilege of designating either life imprisonment or death with a verdict of guilty of murder in the first degree, and they think this might be a reason for the delay

WIDOW EXPECTS TO BE SET FREE

Friday, 10/27/1916 (*Bridgeton Evening News, via United Press*). Mrs. Beutinger expects to be set free before nightfall and to clasp her five children to her — cleared of the charge of murder.

A POSITIVE FEELING

Saturday, 10/28/1916 (*New York Tribune*). After the jury retired, Mrs. Beutinger kept asking "I wonder why they are so long?" according to Miss Florence Bell, a court attendant. "I am sure they will acquit me."

JURY OUT EIGHT HOURS, IS LOCKED UP

Saturday, 10/28/1916 (*New York Sun*). When the twelve jurors filed out of the box this afternoon, nearly every spectator believed they would return within half an hour.

Mrs. Beutinger, in a separate room with attendant Florence Bell, was certain of quick vindication. Her five little children were told that Mama would be home for supper. An automobile waited in front of the courthouse for the intended triumphal return to Caldwell.

Finally, the children became hungry. They were fed dinner, and, after waiting a while in the courtroom, they grew sleepy, and they were taken to the automobile and tucked in robes so they could sleep. A crowd of a hundred or more people stood solemnly looking at them through the automobile windows.

Margaret, the oldest at age 8, felt something was wrong. She refused to be budged from her courtroom seat. But at last she succumbed, and she left a final message: "Tell Mama we'll have a party waiting when she comes home."

7. Autumn 1916

JURY ASKS FOR INSTRUCTIONS

Saturday, 10/28/1916 (*The New York Evening World*). The jury was first heard from at 9 o'clock this morning when it submitted two questions to the Court. The first was:

- "If a defendant desires to establish self-defense, does the law impose the necessity of taking all reasonable steps to avert the tragedy?"

In reply, the Court said: "If she had a reasonable opportunity to retreat, the law would require that she do so."
The next question was:

- "Should a person avoid a situation of circumstances which would require self-defense?"

The Court answered this, saying:

"That would depend on the circumstances. A person should not deliberately create such a situation, but if one arose, the law would not prevent a person from exercising the right of self-defense. If the defendant herself created such a situation, she could not exercise that right."

DOES WOMAN HAVE CONTROL OVER HER BODY?
By Carl D. Groat, United Press

Saturday, 10/28/1916 *(Salem, Oregon, Daily Capital Journal)*. When the jury went into deliberations at 3:05 yesterday afternoon, Mrs. Beutinger was confident of acquittal. Throughout the night the jurors wrangled over the question:

"Has a married woman, the mother of five children, the right of ownership of her own body and the right to kill, if necessary, to protect it?"

After 18 hours of deliberation, the jury came in at 9:23 this morning and submitted two more questions to the court:

1. "Does the law impose upon the defendant the necessity of taking all reasonable steps to avert a tragedy when she wishes to establish a plea of self-defense?"

2. "Please define again the different degrees of homicide."

The first question evidently arose from the judge's instructions yesterday that to establish self-defense the defense must show that Mrs. Beutinger had retreated if she had had an opportunity to do so.

Her lawyer had objected to that portion of the charge on the ground that she was lying down and was unable to retreat.

In response to the jurors' question, Judge Martin gave a more detailed, technical answer, citing court decisions.

The second question tended to confirm speculation that some jurors are refusing to acquit the defendant but are holding out for some kind of punishment.

IMPOSSIBLE TO AGREE

Saturday, 10/28/1916 *(New York Evening World)*. "This case has aroused great public interest, I know," warned Judge Martin just before the jury returned, "but no matter what may be done it is highly undesirable that either approval or disapproval be shown."

Mrs. Beutinger was then brought in, pale, but without tears and leaning on the arm of matron Bell. She fell into a seat at the side of the court clerk, and immediately dropped her head to her folded arms and sobbed hysterically as the jury entered.

"Gentlemen, have you agreed on a verdict?"

"No, your honor, we cannot agree."

"You have now considered this case for twenty-two hours, and I am sure you have weighed the evidence carefully. You cannot agree. I thank you for your careful consideration, and you are hereby discharged.

"The second trial of the defendant is set for Monday, November 20, at 10 a.m., and she is remanded to the Essex County Jail."

For several seconds there was only the deep sobbing of the prisoner. Then the matron touched her gently on the shoulder, and she arose and returned to the narrow aisle that led to an iron spiral stairway to the sheriff's room.

She broke down completely there and was almost carried out to the van that took her back to jail. Her sister was denied permission to see her.

Defense attorney Brandley said he would apply for bail, which had been promised by a "prominent man" in the community.

It was revealed that Mrs. Beutinger has received a letter from a man who had been a reporter with the *Honolulu, Hawaii, Advertiser*. It read, in part:

"If you are the same little woman who was beaten up that night in Honolulu (1914), you have rid the community of a brute who has no business on Earth, and I feel that any sane jury will quickly acquit you.

"I've handled and reported many wife-beating cases, but never saw a woman so badly beaten up as this one was."

During her direct testimony yesterday, Mrs. Beutinger had referred in detail to a beating she had suffered at the Moana Hotel in Honolulu. It was afterward that her husband signed a pledge to abstain from liquor and from violence toward her.

The promise, she testified, was soon broken.

JURORS AMAZE BY SPLITTING

Sunday, 10/29/1916 (*New York Sun*). Judging from what was said around the courthouse in Newark, in the streets, and in the shops — everywhere — the two men on the jury who stood against freeing Mrs. Beutinger were the only ones in town who thought that way.

"They'll take twenty minutes to acquit her" was the murmur that sounded all over the courtroom on Friday when the jury filed out. But twenty-two hours later the jury was back, haggard and unshaven, to say they could not reach a decision.

The first ballot had stood at ten for acquittal and two for conviction of manslaughter. The next vote was eleven for conviction on manslaughter and one for acquittal.

Manslaughter is the crime of killing someone without malice, or ill will, and it normally carries a lesser punishment.

Another ballot at 10 a.m. is reported to have shown ten for acquittal and two for manslaughter, and it stood that way until the end.

As the judge left for lunch after he had set the case for retrial in November, he expressed himself in disgusted tones.

"No, the jury didn't do anything," he observed. "They were in there twenty-two hours, and I thought they'd do something, but they didn't."

Defense attorney Brandley was with Mrs. Beutinger for half an hour, and the burden of her talk was —

"Have it fixed so that I can see my children," she begged him over and over.

The lack of a jury decision was a great shock, but it did not shake her faith that she would be set free. She is eager for a new trial, the attorney said.

The sympathy for the woman came from all classes of people.

A prominent Newark lawyer entered the courtroom just after the trial ended.

"Where's the jury?" he asked.

"Gone out the back door."

"That's the way they ought to go," the lawyer growled.

Two old negro women halted some reporters on the courthouse steps. "How did the poor lady come out in her trouble?"

"It was a hung jury," they were told. They seemed shocked.

One court official who had heard some of Mrs. Beutinger's testimony said the only fault he found with her is that she "didn't kill her husband a long time before."

DEFENDANT IS HEART-BROKEN

Monday, 10/31/1916 (*Trenton Evening Times*). Heart-broken over the jury's failure to acquit her, Mrs. Beutinger has issued the following statement through her attorneys:

"It came to me like a bolt from a clear sky — the announcement by the foreman that the jury had disagreed.

"I regard the failure of those 12 men as an injustice to a mother who has borne seven children and who has forgiven so often so much ill treatment and abuse.

"It is especially hard now, when I am left practically penniless with my children. Their disappointment at my inability to join them in Caldwell is my greatest pain, for I have given my whole life to and for them.

"This is a case of the abuse of the birthright of a woman to defend her life at whatever cost, though I feel that nothing can stand in the way of my eventually being cleared of blame."

WOMEN ARE INDIGNANT

Sunday, 10/29/1916 (*Trenton Evening Times*). Judge Martin discharged the jury yesterday afternoon.

It had rejected the idea that a married woman had the right to protect herself from her husband's unwelcome advances by taking his life, but it had failed to agree on the degree of homicide.

Report has it that the jurors stood 10 to 2 for man-

SLAYER OF HUSBAND WHOSE JURY FAILED TO REACH AN AGREEMENT.

Mrs. MARGARET C. BEUTINGER
Photographed at Essex County Jail

slaughter, with some jurors opting for probation and others wanting 10 years' imprisonment.

Women who attended the trial were indignant at the

failure of the jury to bring in a prompt acquittal. They had been confident that Mrs. Beutinger's story would win her freedom. Any jury of women would have brought in a "not guilty" verdict, they said, without even leaving the jury box.

In a retrial of the case, a new witness may be a Honolulu reporter who wrote to Mrs. Beutinger and backed up her story of having been beaten at a Honolulu hotel two years ago.

TWO JURORS SOUGHT GUILTY VERDICT

Monday, 10/30/1916 (*Trenton Evening Times*). It was learned that during the early part of the jury's 22 hours of deliberations, ten of the jurors were for acquittal, but the other two voted to convict of murder in the first degree.

The sentence for first-degree murder could have been death or life in prison.

Subsequently the ten announced that they would vote for manslaughter if the two would cease to advocate for the murder verdict. Their plan was to then argue for acquittal after the obdurate two had assented to the lesser charge.

One enterprising newspaper writer sought out the opinion of a widely known, controversial New York woman lawyer, Lucille Pugh (pictured), who was in the habit of wearing men's attire in court — except for the trousers; she donned a skirt.

A feminist when that term had not been invented, she condemned the "unmanliness" of the men on the jury and added:

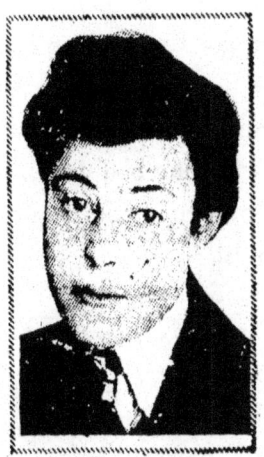
Lucille Pugh

WOMAN LAWYER ASSAILS JURY

Sunday, 10/29/1916 (*Trenton Evening Times*). "If killing a man is the only way a woman can protect herself against his sensuous assault, then I say kill him.

"From what I can learn of the evidence, this little woman did right in stopping that brute's advance with a bullet.

"With the evidence showing her in a battered condition as she lay in bed, it is inconceivable how any judge and jury could for an instant blame her for killing the man who insisted on approaching her.

"It is astounding that in this presumably enlightened twentieth century there should be any question about a woman owning and controlling her own body.

"My experience as a lawyer among women shows me that there are thousands of them who spend their lives in seeking a solution to the problem faced by Mrs. Beutinger.

"The peculiar thing is that more men do not meet the fate that he met.

"If I had a husband like that, I would either by myself — or by a proxy — scare him badly with a good beating so he would leave me alone, then take him by the nape of the neck and kick him out!"

Meanwhile, Mrs. B was returned to her jail cell, where ten days later she received a very odd visit from an Essex County elected official. You get the details of this tacky encounter after the next chapter, which sets the stage.

8. Beer Fountains and Votes for Women

New Jersey is the fourth-smallest state in the Union, with frontage on the Atlantic Ocean and backage on the Delaware River.

There are twenty-one counties in New Jersey, Essex being one of the four oldest, founded in 1683 and proud of that fact.

In the early years of the last century, the town of Caldwell was considered—

HISTORIC BUT PROGRESSIVE

Sunday, 9/6/1914 (*New York Tribune*). One of the most rapidly growing towns in the suburban district of New Jersey is Caldwell, just twenty miles from the heart of New York City. It has a population of about three thousand.

Caldwell is a hilltop town, some 600 feet above sea level, sheltered on the east by the Orange Mountains, while to the west the plateau drops by a sweeping descent into a great valley through which, broken by graceful undulations, the Passaic River stretches for nine miles to the blue line of the Hook Mountain and the foothills of the Blue Ridge.

It has a delightful climate. The never-failing western breezes are free in the summer from depressing humidity, and in the winter the air is crisp and dry, like the Adirondacks, so the coldest days are stimulating and enjoyable.

Caldwell is also gaining favor as a summer town; the New York City residents who seek its pleasures during the warm days of summer usually return the following year and for many years thereafter.

The town has fine roads, cement sidewalks, water and gas mains, electric light, and police and fire protection. Model sewerage and disposal plants have been installed. The water supply, from artesian wells, is absolutely pure. There are excellent public and private schools, churches of various denominations, a public library, a lively newspaper, two national banks, garages, and good shops of all sorts.

There is free delivery from New York and Newark department stores.

Night or day, the community is within easy traveling distance of New York. If a traveler cannot get home at night by an Erie train, he can go to Montclair over the Lackawanna Railroad and thence by trolley to his destination, four miles to the west.

Many people live in Caldwell and work in Newark, a trolley ride of about ten miles in distance and an hour in duration. The fare is 10 cents.

NO TROLLEY WIRES FOR STREETCAR LINE

Thursday, 1/27/1910 (*East Liverpool, Ohio, Evening Review*). Caldwell, New Jersey, is to have the country's first line of trolleyless street cars on eight miles of track. Plans are under way to substitute the storage battery for the wire-arm. All eyes will be leveled on that town.

BEER FOUNTAINS PROPOSED IN CALDWELL

Friday, 10/15/1915 (*Hagerstown, Maryland, Morning Herald*). CALDWELL, New Jersey, October 14 — The Town Council of Caldwell received a shock when the Caldwell Lager and Beer Company, through its secretary-treasurer, Lester Schmit, presented a petition to that august body asking for the privilege of building a porcelain-lined tank, with a capacity of not less than 500 barrels of beer, on top of Caldwell Mountain.

The expressions of surprise on the faces of the councilmen changed to horror when, farther down in the petition, it was stated that the company desired to lay pipes under the streets, so as to supply the homes of its patrons with a limitless quantity of beer fresh from the tank, The object was stated to be reducing the cost of water rents to the residents by increasing the consumption of beer.

The petitioner also asked for the privilege of erecting beer fountains in the city parks and streets, so that thirsty citizens could drop a nickel in a slot and get a glass of fresh beer without the necessity of going to New York.

To show the liberal spirit of the petitioner, the offer was made to erect such a fountain in the council chamber for the use of the council members, at no charge.

After the petition was read aloud, the council gravely referred it to a committee for action, or lack thereof.

All this is very amusing — or somewhat amusing — but there was serious stuff going on as well.

New Jersey was the first state in the East to submit to the voters a state constitutional amendment authorizing women's suffrage (the right to vote), in 1915. Despite a hard-fought campaign, it was resoundingly defeated by the all-male electorate. Some of the defeat, it was said, was caused by the required closing of all saloons on election day, giving customers nothing to do with their time except go out and vote against women.

SUFFRAGE CARRIED ONLY ONE COUNTY

Wednesday, 10/20/1915 (*The New York Times*). There can be no doubt of the decisive sentiment against the enfranchisement of women among the voters in New Jersey. Every county but one, Ocean County, went solidly against the state constitutional amendment.

Essex County was against suffrage by a majority estimated at 10,000, the largest in the history of that county, and certainly the largest in proportion to the total vote cast in any election ever held in New Jersey.

President Wilson's endorsement of the suffrage cause, upon which the suffragists had placed such high hopes, did not help. Even the precinct in Princeton Borough where he voted went against the measure.

Even as the president was on his way to Princeton to vote, his fiancée, Mrs. Edith Bolling Galt, let it be known in Washington that she is opposed to women voting. *(The president and Mrs. Galt were married two months later despite their difference over women's suffrage.)*

The suffragists found the great political machines arrayed against them, but the women put up strenuous and unfaltering battle and managed to get out a heavy vote.

The real storm center was in Essex County, where the forces of James R. Nugent, the Democratic leader, were openly opposed to women's suffrage. The state's unexpectedly heavy voting was especially noticeable in Essex; all of Newark seemed to be tensely alive. It was more like a Presidential contest than a special election on a constitutional amendment.

Complaints came into suffrage headquarters from Nugent-controlled districts that women were not receiving courteous treatment at the polling places, where the women were on watch. Men at the polls delighted in assuming a facetious attitude toward them, declining to give serious answers to their questions. Several women were offended and wanted to quit, but by far the greater number were defiant and eager to show the men that they could stand their ground.

NUGENT'S SATIRIC COMMENT

Wednesday, 10/20/1915 (*The New York Times*). James R. Nugent, Democratic leader who led the anti-suffrage forces in Essex County, expressed great satisfaction over the results.

He said the anti-suffrage campaign had been directed by the best citizenship and womanhood of the State, but the other side was the work of a coterie of imported, hysterical, itinerant reformers and female politicians. *(There's that word again — "hysterical.")*

"The strongest argument presented by the sober-minded Jersey men against woman suffrage," he said, "has been a procession of long-haired men and short-haired women streaming across the Hudson River from New York into New Jersey" in support of the suffrage amendment.

9. Freeholder Ryman

On Tuesday, November 7, 1916, New Jerseyans went to the polls. They voted to re-elect President Woodrow Wilson, who lived in South Jersey. They also voted on local offices, including the Board of Chosen Freeholders, the governing body of Essex County.

Ernest E. Ryman, the director, or chairman, of the board, was re-elected. He was pretty happy (and drunk) as the next day he made an official visit with other freeholders to inspect the County Jail.

TAUNTED, THEN HIT HER, SHE SAYS

Thursday, 11/16/1916 (*New York Tribune*). Ernest E. Ryman, director of the Board of Freeholders of Essex County, was held yesterday on a warrant charging assault and battery on Margaret C. Beutinger.

He is accused of visiting the County Jail and taunting the imprisoned woman by telling her that he would never acquit her if he were on a jury to try her.

Mrs. Beutinger also asserts that on Wednesday, November 8 *(the day after the election)* he struck her on the knee with his fist.

RYMAN PLEADS NOT GUILTY

Wednesday, 11/15/1916 (*Newark Evening News*). As an outcome of his visit to Mrs. Beutinger's jail cell on November 8, Director Ryman was held in bail of $500 for the grand jury on a charge of assault and battery against her.

Accompanied by his counsel, Assemblyman Edward Schoen, Ryman appeared before Judge William F. Martin and pleaded not guilty. His bail was furnished by Ernest G. Stauber.

Mrs. Beutinger, a jail matron, and two other women prisoners were brought to the courthouse to speak to Judge Martin. The unusual haste in taking up the case, on the same day of Ryman's not-guilty plea, was under Martin's direct order.

Investigations have been conducted independently by Martin and by County Prosecutor Jacob L. Newman.

Attorney Shoen made the following statement on Ryman's behalf:

"The complaint is an afterthought, and Mr. Ryman denies it absolutely.

"Originally, Mrs. Beutinger merely claimed that Mr. Ryman had spoken harshly to her. It took several days to evolve the form of the present complaint. The fact that Mrs. Beutinger is to go to trial again on Monday makes glaringly apparent the motive for the complaint at this time." *(His intimation was that her complaint was just a ruse to gain sympathy.)*

The woman's formal statement yesterday brought the first definite charge that Ryman had touched her. It stated that he took hold of her by force and that he struck her upon the knee.

Ryman was an important politician, so others in the town rallied to his defense. It was difficult for a judge to even get a grand jury to indict him, as you can see from the next story.

JAILED WOMAN MUST BE PROTECTED

Thursday, 11/16/1916 (*Newark Evening News*). The grand jury was summoned this afternoon before Judge William P. Martin, who called its attention to the charge of assault and battery made against Freeholders Director Ernest E. Ryman.

The judge told the jurors they should consider the charge without considering the unfortunate position of the complainant *(that is, being a jailed inmate suspected of murder)* nor the effect that their action might be expected to have on her second trial.

That she was facing a serious charge, he said, did not remove her from the protection of the law, and she should be protected from outrage or insult of any kind, just as any free woman in the county.

He considered it unfortunate that this case might cause undue sympathy to arise for the woman, but the grand jury had no control over that.

The judge explained that the crime of assault and battery did not necessarily require bodily injury to result.

This means that the mere touching of somebody could be an assault.

The judge described a visit to Mrs. Beutinger's room by Ryman while she was thinly clad and, according to her complaint, her visitor put his hand on her arm and later on her knee. The judge reminded the jury that the inmate was a charge of the county and must be protected from affronts of any kind.

HISTORY OF ALLEGED ASSAULT

Friday, 11/24/1916 (*Newark Evening News*). By the bare minimum vote needed, the grand jury returned an indictment yesterday regarding the affront said to have been offered Mrs. Beutinger by Selectman Ryman in the County Jail on November 8.

The judge had summoned the grand jury into his chambers last week and in no uncertain terms said it was its right, if not its duty, to indict Ryman. But even this charge did not bring immediate action by the jurors.

In the end, twelve of the twenty grand jurors voted for the indictment, the minimum necessary.

RYMAN SAYS HE IS INNOCENT

Thursday, 12/14/1916 (*Asbury Park, New Jersey, Press*). Ryman entered a plea of not guilty when he was arraigned on a charge of assault and battery.

The news caused a storm of protest against Ryman, like this—

EDITORIAL OPINION

Monday, 1/3/1917 (*Newark Evening News*). It is intolerable that any woman held in the County Jail, whether because of misfortune or misconduct, should be compelled to submit to insult from a person who, because of the accident of office, is permitted the freedom of that institution.

Until Mrs. Beutinger's guilt has been proven to the satisfaction of a 12-man jury, she is innocent in the eyes of the law. Thus far that proof has not been presented.

Director Ryman had just been re-elected to office. Probably, as the saying goes, he was "feeling his oats." This may explain but cannot excuse his insult of a helpless woman whose situation at least entitles her to some pity.

Ryman should have the grace to apologize for his conduct.

A month later, the trial began.

FREEHOLDER GOT FRESH, INMATE SAYS

Thursday, 2/6/1917 (*New York Tribune*). Mrs. Beutinger testified about Ryman's visit on November 8, just after a jury had disagreed at her first trial, with the woman ill in bed when he entered her cell and the matron introduced him.

She asserted that he was intoxicated and attempted to caress her. After his first call, he returned with a friend

Ryman admitted he had been drinking when he made his jail inspection. He said that he might have patted her hand.

I am sure he might have — in an avuncular way, of course. Here are more details from other newspapers.

PROSECUTION BEGINS IN RYMAN CASE

Friday, 2/7/1917 (*Newark Evening News*). Mrs. Beutinger testified that Ryman told her:

"Had I been on the jury, I would have voted for your conviction."

Hearing this, she began to cry, and she told Ryman that if he had read the accounts in the papers he would not have felt as he did.

"I then said to him that I wouldn't kill an ant unless it were to protect myself."

This remark provoked the following from Ryman:

"I'm sorry. I didn't think you were such a little woman. I am surprised to see you are so small and so good-looking. If I had known this, I would have changed my mind about voting for your conviction."

She continued:

"Ryman pulled my hand toward him and pressed it to his face. I resisted and realized he had been drinking, as I smelled liquor on his breath. I asked him if he had a mother, and if he would like her to see him in such a condition. He replied he would not."

She said Ryman stayed about fifteen minutes, went away, and when he returned he pushed her knees down as she lay in bed. He left, returned a third time with a man and asked if he might introduce a friend. The warden's wife then announced that dinner was ready, and they left.

In his cross-examination, defense attorney Alexander

Simpson indicated that the incident was not a serious one and was made only to arouse sympathy for Mrs. Beutinger.

More than that, Simpson attempted to obtain an admission that Mrs. Beutinger had placed a flower in the buttonhole of Ryman's coat. She admitted that she had asked the matron to take two flowers from a vase and give one to Ryman, but she said she did so only to hasten his departure.

Was it true, Simpson asked, if the jail matron had chided her for "kidding and carrying on" under such circumstances? She replied that nothing of the kind had been said.

The defense lawyer became a bit too edgy with Mrs. B for the judge's taste.

Simpson asked Mrs. Beutinger several times if she did not want all the sympathy and help she could get and if she were not well enough acquainted with court procedure to know the effect that sympathy would have on her forthcoming trial.

County Prosecutor Newman objected, and Judge Osborne warned Simpson: "Do not continue asking questions along that line if you wish to continue in this case."

Emma Reynolds, a girl who had been at the jail awaiting sentence, corroborated most of Mrs. Beutinger's testimony as to Ryman's holding her hand and talking to her.

Anna Selsby, who was Mrs. Beutinger's cellmate, said she saw Ryman sitting by Mrs. Beutinger's bedside, but it appeared to her that the man's actions were done in a spirit of "playfulness." Mrs. Beutinger did complain to the jail matron, Mrs. Fish, who responded: "Oh, that's only his jovial way."

Dr. Edward Markens, the jail physician, said that Mrs. Beutinger was hysterical when he was called to treat her that night.

DEFENSE GIVES ITS SIDE

Friday, 2/7/1917 (*Newark Evening News*). Jerome T. Congelton, Ryman's lawyer, began the defense presentation at 3 in the afternoon.

County Supervisor Lewis G. Bowden was the first witness for the defense. He said he was with Ryman and saw him holding Mrs. Beutinger's hand. She made no effort to release herself, and therefore he thought nothing about it.

"Was Ryman feeling good?" defense attorney Newman asked. *(An odd way to ask it, but the witness knew what was meant.)*

Bowden said he believed Ryman had been drinking, adding: "Anyone who knows him can tell pretty nearly by looking at him whether he's been drinking."

Ryman himself took the stand and said it was Mrs. Beutinger who took the initiative in the hand-holding, not he, and the only time she showed distress was after he declared that he might have voted for conviction had he been on the jury.

He said she had extended her hand in greeting, and

then she asked if Ryman thought she should have been acquitted. "'I don't know,' I said. 'If I had been on the jury, I wouldn't have voted to acquit you.' This started to make her feel bad."

Another newspaper reported that Ryman had told her she should be sent to the electric chair.

Ryman was unable to recount the talk that followed, describing it only as a rambling sort of conversation. "When I left, she bid me goodbye and put a little flower in my coat."

He said that Mrs. Beutinger held fast to his hand for a considerable time; he denied that she tried to pull it away. "If she did, she could have done so."

He also denied he pushed her knees down from their bent position.

He said he tried to make amends for the thoughtless remark he passed about the jury, telling her that she need not cry because she probably would be cleared in the second trial. He offered to do anything he could for her.

Under attorney Newman's cross-examination, Ryman denied he was intoxicated during the visit. He was happy over his reelection but had taken only a few drinks in the morning and nothing in the afternoon. Pressed to remember the exact number, he said he might have had five, although "I don't really count them."

He said he came back a second time to introduce his friend, Ernest G. Stauber, "to show him what a nice woman she was."

Mrs. Fish, the matron, testified that she had observed nothing particularly wrong in Ryman's actions, although she considered his sitting by the bed and holding her hand to be unusual.

Nellie Noonan, Mrs. Beutinger's cellmate, testified that she heard Anna Silsby, another inmate who was acting in the capacity of nurse, tell Mrs. Beutinger that she had been foolish to let him hold her hand, to be so free with her, because he would just go out and tell all the other Freeholders about it. Then Mrs. Beutinger buried her face in the bedclothes, crying, and moaned that with *everything* she did she "put her heart into it."

Mrs. Beutinger's trial attorney, Walter Brandley, testified that Ryman had told him after the election that he was so drunk when he visited the jail that he did not remember what had occurred.

There were a number of character witnesses for Ryman, including a sheriff's lieutenant, a tax commissioner, and a police commissioner. This guy was really powerful in the corruption stew of North Jersey.

JURY CANNOT AGREE

Wednesday, 2/7/1917 (*Newark Evening News*). The jury in the Ryman trial was hopelessly deadlocked and has been discharged.

At 9:40 in the evening, a note was sent from the jury room declaring there was no hope of agreement. William Crowther, clerk of the court, telephoned Judge Osborne at his home and was instructed to discharge the jury.

It was rumored that the vote was eight for acquittal and four for conviction.

This case was never retried.

10. The Second Trial

In the days when women of quality did not go out to work, they might occupy themselves with their choice of a woman's club, and there were quite a few clubwomen interested in Mrs. Beutinger, who was much like them.

CLUBWOMEN PETITION FOR SLAYER

Sunday, 11/12/1916 (*New York Tribune*). Clubwomen of Montclair and Caldwell are circulating a petition to be presented to Judge William P. Martin asking for the release on bail of Margaret Claire Beutinger, who is being held for the killing of her husband, pending her second trial, set for November 20.

Mrs. Nelson B. Chester, wife of the pastor of the Presbyterian Church at Caldwell, presented the petition at the anniversary meeting of the Pen and Point Circle in the home of Mrs. W.G. Sharwell, and it was signed by the sixty women present.

It has also been signed by members of the Half-Hour Reading Club, the Ray Palmer Club, the Isabella Literary

Club of Verona, the All Round Club of Montclair, the Roseland Women's Club, and the Caldwell Borough Improvement Association.

Mrs. B had been allowed to see her children in the County Jail outside her cell, but for some reason that privilege was revoked the day after a grand jury indicted Ernest E. Ryman for assault and battery against her. Go figure.

HINT COURT TEST OF CHILDREN BAN

Friday, 11/24/1916 (*Newark Evening News*). There were indications today that a court test may be made of the sheriff's order barring Mrs. Beutinger the privilege of seeing her five children except through prison bars.

The first move came when Mrs. Jennie Herron, sister of the accused, brought the children to the jail just before noon. She was accompanied by Mrs. Beutinger's attorney, Walter Brandley.

Mrs. Beutinger refused to see her little ones if they had to be brought to her cell. She formerly was able to see them either in Warden McGuinness's office or the Freeholders' committee room, but that privilege was ended by an order from the sheriff's office after she filed her charge against Ryman.

Warden McGuinness informed the two that the rules of the institution required that people charged with a capital crime must be visited in their cell. He made no reference to the previous order by the sheriff.

Brandley sought unsuccessfully to communicate with either Sheriff Schmidt or the undersheriff, Conrad Deuchler. He and Mrs. Herron and the children then simply waited.

There was no word on the outcome of this family sit-in. Instead, the newspapers turned their attention to Mrs. B's second trial.

HARD-FOUGHT BATTLE IS SEEN

Tuesday, 12/5/1916 (*New York Tribune*). Looking like a schoolgirl who had come up for her examinations, but with her five little children in a row behind her, Mrs. Margaret Claire Beutinger went on trial yesterday for a second time.

It is evident that this trial will be harder fought than the first in that prosecutor Newman has introduced a new theory — that Mrs. Beutinger shot her husband not while protecting herself from his brutality but rather as he sat quietly in a chair.

That fact was proven by the bloodstains upon the back of a rocking chair and the fact that the bullets took a downward path through the victim's body, he contended.

Another new element was brought in by defense attorney Robert H. McCarter asking potential jurors if any had been prejudiced by the indictment of Board of Freeholders

THE BATTERED WIFE

MRS. BEUTINGER EXPECTS ACQUITAL

CALDWELL, N. J., WOMAN WHO SHOT AND KILLED HUSBAND EXPECTS TO BE FREED OF CHARGE AT SECOND TRIAL

Mrs. Margaret C. Beutinger and her five children.

member Ernest E. Ryman on a charge of assault and battery in her cell on November 8.

The incident has brought the issue of politics into the trial, and that circumstance has won some sympathy for the defendant, but at the same time it has made her many enemies on account of Ryman's power and influence.

One potential juror did admit that the Ryman incident had biased him against the prisoner, and he was excused.

When the defendant was brought into the room by court attendant Mary Kelly, her little son, Fred, 7 years old, ran within the railing and cast himself upon her. His mother made the most in hugs and kisses before others came forward for the child.

Mrs. Beutinger begged to be united with her children at noon, but Undersheriff Conrad Deuchler replied with an emphatic "No!" She has not seen any of them since the last trial because she refused to talk with them from behind cell bars.

She seems now to have shaken off some of the sorrow and stupor that oppressed her during the first trial. She sat alert and tense between her lawyers, not missing one point of the prosecution's theory and leaning forward to whisper suggestions.

Her eyes softened as she turned now and then to meet those of her children. Billy, the baby, fell asleep, but the others tossed kisses every time she looked at them, and they took turns watching her through opera glasses.

DEFENDANT HAS BRIGHT, NEW LOOK

Tuesday, 12/5/1916 (*New York Sun*). Margaret Beutinger is a different figure during this trial. In the last court skirmish, she wore a not very becoming dress and hat *(certainly a different description from what we read earlier)*, and she sat apathetically beside the court attendant, taking little notice of the proceedings and apparently not seeing much besides the glimpses of her children on the other side of the room.

This time she is wearing a trim little blue serge dress with a broad, white satin collar and cuffs, and she sports a white "Tommy Atkins" hat atop her prettily arranged dark hair.

All day, alert and keen-eyed, she consulted with her attorneys and suggested questions, watching jurors, missing no point.

She had discarded the sombre mourning she wore in October. She was eager, by the way, that the newspaper people should know that the mourning was not for her husband, but for her mother, who died last year.

When she reentered the courtroom after noon recess, she had removed her hat, and some of the spectators opened their eyes when they saw how much like a girl she looked. Her abundant, soft black hair was drawn high at the back, there was faint color in her crystalline face, and unless one looked straight at her and saw the deep circles under the eyes, it was hard to realize that she is a mother of many children and a woman who has known much suffering.

The jury was selected very quickly, in just one hour. Thirty of the panel were rejected before twelve were chosen.

The visit of Ernest E. Ryman, director of the Board of Freeholders, to Mrs. Beutinger's cell and his indictment on a charge of assaulting her cropped up at once, to the dismay of prosecutor Newman. He protested when defense attorney McCarter asked a prospective juror, George Lee, if he knew Ryman and if the affair would affect his judgment. Lee said it would not, but he was excused anyway.

William Noble, a mild-looking elderly man, accountant by profession, is the foreman. Charles Brautigan, retired butcher, is No. 2. The third man chosen, William Graves, admitted frankly that he had "a prejudice in favor of the defense" but he was sure he could decide according to the evidence. Charles Hill of East Orange, the only juror not living in Newark, said he had "no opinion, but a sympathetic feeling," and at that Mrs. Beutinger nodded in satisfaction as he was accepted.

SYMPATHY AROUSED BY INDICTMENT

Monday, 12/4/1916 (*New York Evening World*). The publicity over the indictment of E.E. Ryman of the Essex County Board of Freeholders has created much sentiment in favor of Mrs. Beutinger, which became more evident during the questioning of the potential jurors.

The jurors selected are William Noble, accountant; Charles Brautigan, retired butcher; William Graves, manufacturer; Frank H. Brewster, clerk; Miles G. Burns, cigar manufacturer; Edwin E. Wilcox, New York Fire Exchange; L. Tracy Mills, life insurance; Charles F. Manning, clerk; Charles Hill, merchant; Grant Goodwin, salesman; Gustave S. Hauff, engraver, and Robert F. Telfer, clerk.

DEFENDANT NEAR COLLAPSE

Tuesday, 12/5/1916 (*New York Evening World*). Mrs.

Beutinger testified, as she had at her first trial, that she never suspected her husband's drinking habit and was greatly surprised when they were on their honeymoon, in Washington, and he came home intoxicated and made her get up and entertain friends he brought with him.

She told of a similar experience in Chicago, where, she said, her husband took her into a bathroom and threatened her with his razor because she had said she might tell the War Department of his grafting operations in Manila.

When noon recess was taken, Mrs. Beutinger was bordering on collapse. She had to be almost carried from the courtroom by Miss Kelly, her guard, and her moans could be heard for some time after she was taken upstairs.

DRUNK ON SECOND DAY OF MARRIAGE

Wednesday, 12/6/1916 (*Trenton Evening Times*). Margaret Beutinger told how her husband had threatened her with a razor and with a pen knife, how he had beaten her with a poker, and how, in Manila he dragged her by the hair from a ballroom floor before a thousand observers because, unknowingly, she had danced with an officer who had given information against Beutinger when he was removed from the Quartermaster's Department in the Army on charges of graft.

'MAMA, LET'S GO BACK'

Wednesday, 12/6/1916 (*New York Tribune*). Mrs. Beutinger said that she returned to her husband last Christmas despite her fear because her children begged her. He had promised them a Christmas tree, she said.

"I was afraid," she sobbed, "but the children begged, 'Please, Mama, let's go back.'"

In this way, she disposed of the argument that is said to have counted against her most strongly in the first trial — that she consented to live with him again.

She also told for the first time why she did not lock her bedroom doors against him.

"I was afraid to lock them. He might have broken one of them in, as he had done before, and then it would have been all the harder for me."

Mrs. Beutinger said the Mother Superior of St. Clare Convent and the Bishop of Jamaica had told her it was a duty to the church to remarry, and the final straw came when the children begged her to "take papa back."

The next two articles were printed two months later, in Hawaii, but I am placing them here to keep chronology.

HONEYMOON TRIP HELPED DEFENDANT

Friday, 2/16/1917 (*Hawaiian Gazette*). An echo of a scandal, aired in Honolulu several years ago, has been brought back here by a passenger on the transport *Logan*, now in port — Casimir N. Guertin, of the Philippines secret service.

The Honolulu police, and the public generally, have a vivid recollection of the brutal assault made on Mrs. Margaret Claire Beutinger by her husband in the Moana Hotel in June 1914.

Through a strange fancy of fate, Guertin, who was on his honeymoon with his bride, the former Ruby Williams, reached the East Coast at the time when Mrs. Beutinger was on trial for her life in Newark.

He went there immediately; the defendant recognized him in court, and he was qualified as a witness.

SUPPORTS HER STORY

Wednesday, 2/14/1917 (*Honolulu Star-Bulletin*). A man stood up in the courtroom. He was tall, soldierly, and faultlessly dressed.

Casimir N. Guertin corroborated Mrs. Beutinger's account, averring that he had seen Beutinger assault the defendant in Manila and drag her from the ballroom.

LETTER FROM GERMANY

Tuesday, 12/12/1916 (*Kingston Gleaner*). A letter to

Christof Beutinger from his aged mother, living in Germany, was introduced as evidence.

"How much sorrow and heartache you have caused us," his mother wrote. "I do not like to go among people for fear they will ask about you. I do not understand how a man with common sense can lead such a life.

"There is still time for you. I beg for you daily that the dear Christ may give you strength to lead a new, God-fearing life and that your wife and children will be united again. How sorry I feel for those poor, innocent children, who are so much attached to their father.

"Margaret wrote in her last letter that if we should pray for you perhaps you would behave yourself."

The letter closed by asking him to read a hymn that his mother had taught to him in childhood.

TWO MORE WITNESSES

Thursday, 12/7/1916 (*New York Tribune*). Two witnesses testified against Christof Beutinger.

"He told me that he would be tempted to kill her unless she came back to him, so I advised her to go," said Sister Catherine, Mother Superior of the Convent of St. Clare, in Mount Hope. "I don't remember that I told her what he had said, but I did urge her to marry him again."

Another witness, Anita M. Swazey, testified that in 1914 she occupied a room next to that of the Beutingers in the Bellevue Hotel in Nagasaki, Japan, when she was awakened by screams.

"I heard him threatening to kill her," Mrs. Swazey said. "I could hear him choking her. I rapped on the wall and said: 'I'll call the police if you don't stop!' After that I didn't hear any more."

CHILD COMFORTS DEFENDANT

Thursday, 12/7/1916 (*New York Sun*). The spectators, tightly packed into the room, were wondering if the case could go to the jury tonight. The five tired children went pattering more frequently than usual to the tank of filtered water for the drinks that are one of the few solaces they have in a world they cannot understand.

Their mother sat beside her junior counsel, Walter Brandley, as her other attorney, Robert H. McCarter, gave his summation to the jury. Her small handkerchief became quite wet, and Brandley quietly tucked his big one into her hand.

She struggled hard to control herself, but the children saw, and little Marie stole away from her aunt and whispered in the ear of Mary Kelly, the court attendant, who sat watchfully behind the prisoner.

Miss Kelly bent over Mrs. Beutinger and softly repeated the whisper.

"Marie says, 'Don't cry, Mama.'"

When McCarter reached the end of his summing-up, a most masterly one, he paused for an instant:

"Gentlemen of the jury," he said, resting his hands on the railing in front of the dozen men, "the life of the defendant is in your keeping.

"December is a historic month for her. It was in December, ten years ago, that she, a girl of 18, was married to Christof Beutinger. It was in December one year ago that she remarried him. It is now December. Christmas comes. The Christmas tree is ready. Let her go."

In the silence, before prosecutor Newman could rise with his papers to address the jury, Mrs. Beutinger's strangling cry sounded through the room.

" Oh! I can't — I can't — I can't go on. Oh, God!"

This low cry, coming in choked gasps from the little prisoner, brought the session prematurely to a close

Miss Kelly gathered her into her arms, and the big, blue-uniformed man who swears in the witnesses pressed water to her lips, but she sobbed on, grasping her throat with her hand.

Miss Kelly began to lead her away, but at the door she fell to the floor, and a male attendant picked her up and carried her up the stairs, her cries of "Oh, God! Oh, God!" dying away as the doors were closed.

For a minute the courtroom was quiet. The jurors leaned forward, not a bit like jurors but simply like men who cannot bear to hear a woman weep. Spectators sniffled. Jennie Herron, the defendant's sister, hid her face behind baby Billy's head, and Marie, who seems to be the family comforter, patted her with her tiny hands.

"Don't cry, Aunty," she begged.

After a short consultation at the bench, and as the big clock in the dusky courtroom indicated a quarter to four, Judge Martin announced that the session would be continued tomorrow.

11. The Verdict

A TENSE WAIT

Friday, 12/8/1916 (*New York Sun*). After the jury filed out at the close of the judge's charge at 12 noon, it became an anxious wait of three hours and five minutes that the little prisoner, her sister, her children, and her friends endured. For Mrs. Beutinger, the wait was lightened by the undersheriff's permission to let her children be with her in a neighboring room.

At 3:40 p.m. the twelve men filed into the courtroom, the prisoner was brought in, and she stood at their side, far more composed than yesterday. She clutched a bottle of smelling salts, awaiting the verdict.

"Not guilty!"

Foreman William H. Noble spoke the words quietly, but as soft as they were, they sounded through the old Essex County courtroom, and, despite Judge Martin's prior warning, began a wave of applause that took attendants several minutes to quell.

Mrs. Beutinger, Acquitted of Murder, And Children to Whom She Returns

Left to Right
Top Row
MARGARET, MARIE
FRED, Centre MRS. MARGARET C
BEUTINGER Bottom Row BILLY and CHRISTOF

FREEDOM, DINNER, THEN TO HOME

Friday, 12/8/1916 (*New York Sun*). Mrs. Beutinger sank into a chair, dazed, and then laughed softly, like a pleased child. She leaned her dark tresses against the shoulder of her guard, Mary Kelly, and passed from laughter into tears.

Walter Brandley, her attorney, came down from conferring with the judge; she grasped his hand, broke into a smile, and uttered words of thanks.

She heard her children's excited clamor and, like a football player making his way through the ranks of an opposing team, she dived through the swirling crowd of spectators and then gathered the small ones to her body.

She flung her arms around Jennie Herron, her sister. Her brother-in-law, who had come from the West Indies, kissed her heartily.

One of the first to congratulate Mrs. Beutinger was John H. De Baus, who had come from Washington, D.C., to testify. He testified yesterday that Christof Beutinger had sought to bribe him to fake an affidavit that De Baus had seen her in a compromising position with a man on a steamship.

Then came women friends, from Caldwell and Montclair and other Jersey towns, headed by Mrs. Gordon Smith, a suffragist of Montclair, who has been most active in circulating petitions on behalf of Mrs. Beutinger.

But the little woman was longing to be away, and so she lifted Billy in her arms and sought to struggle through the crowd.

First, though, there was a gathering in Judge Martin's chambers, where the whole family met with the judge and others involved in the case, even Lieutenant Walter Godfrey, chief of detectives, who had made the revolver tests calculated to show guilt, or innocence.

At least a thousand people thronged outside the courthouse. At first they thought Mrs. Beutinger would leave by the High Street entrance, and they crowded there, and then they thought she would exit by the front door, and they swept around to that side.

But only those who chanced to be waiting by the basement door saw the little figure dart out, with her sister and children and servants, and all of them climb into a huge automobile with lawyer Brandley at the wheel.

A lusty cheer went up, and Mrs. Beutinger waved her handkerchief in response.

She and Mrs. Herron and Brandley dined at a restaurant in Newark, sending the children on to their home with Mrs. Louise Graaf, so they would be there to welcome her when she arrived.

"Are you home to stay?" Billy demanded suspiciously as she got out of Brandley's auto. And the little woman flung her arms around all of them and answered that she had come to stay "forever and ever."

Waiting also in welcome was Father Dykman, the Catholic chaplain connected with the Essex County Jail. He has been her spiritual adviser.

She shook hands with all the reporters, and said, "I thank you from my heart for your consideration, but I don't believe I can say any more tonight, only that I am glad, so glad. I'm very tired."

She went through the front door with her children, a rather pathetic figure, free and vindicated, but frail and young, with five little ones looking to her for support.

Down in his office on Market Street, prosecutor Jacob Newman said:

"I had to do my duty. It wasn't pleasant, but I did it. And the jurors did theirs. I'm wholly satisfied."

He smiled and displayed a note he had received from Robert H. McCarter, senior defense attorney, just before the jury went out.

"Jake, whatever happens in this case, you have been fair as well as able. You have performed your duty admirably, and I congratulate you."

Mrs. Beutinger hasn't said whether her troubles made her believe in votes for women, but she did tell Mrs. Gordon Smith of Montclair, who talked to her in her jail cell before her trial began:

"Oh, if I could have some women on the jury! I think only a woman can really understand!"

JURORS PLAY SANTA CLAUS

Tuesday, 12/26/1916 (*New York Tribune*). There are five children in Caldwell who can produce unimpeachable evidence of the reality of twenty-two genuine Santa Clauses.

They were the members of the two juries in the Beutinger case, ten from the first trial and an even dozen from the second.

On Christmas Eve, after curfew had been rung for the younger children, suddenly automobiles began pulling up outside the Beutinger home. Men dismounted from the cars and pulled a large Christmas tree through the snow into the house.

Within minutes, the children's nursery was converted into a fairyland, with the tree in the corner surrounded by myriads of gifts. And, yes, there were piles of candies and other sweets.

The children were all summoned to see the wonderland wrought by the score of Santas.

"I knew it all along!" burst from Margaret.

"A real fire engine!" shouted Billy.

A constant stream of visitors had come into the house the day before and the day of Christmas. The mailman staggered under a load of cards bearing holiday greetings.

"I've been oh, so happy today," Mrs. Beutinger said. "We probably will give up this house, but I can make any place into a home now. I've got my five treasures, and I am well satisfied."

Then she sat and addressed holiday cards to the two jurors who had not appeared among the self-appointed Santas — the men who had voted "guilty" in the first trial. She wrote:

"I hope you have as merry a Christmas as I am having. May you enjoy many, many happy New Year's."

12. Observations

I'd like to give you some of my opinions about this case.
Did Mrs. B plan to kill Christof. No. She sent away for a gun and loaded it, but only to protect herself. But she was fairly certain that she would have to use it; that's why she told the druggist that "something" would happen. She knew her husband would attack her when she told him she was going to divorce him.

• • •

Mrs. B should have been granted bail, so she didn't have to sit steaming in a jail cell all during a hot New Jersey summer.
Bail is supposed to insure the appearance of a suspect for trial; it is not supposed to be a way to punish an offender in advance of a decision by a jury. It is really hard to see how Mrs. B, with five children to lug around, could have fled the country to avoid trial.
Yes, New Jersey law forbade the posting of bail in a capital case (one in which the punishment could be death), but judges have been known to overturn unjust laws before, and a brave and thoughtful jurist could have done it here as well.

THE BATTERED WIFE

• • •

It's my opinion that no discredit should be cast upon the two jurors who held out for conviction in the first trial. They were simply following the judge's instructions. It was obvious during the jurors' deliberations that these dozen doughty male New Jerseyans were honestly trying to determine exactly what the law was in their state.

I am always amazed when people who have not sat through a trial and heard the evidence and watched the demeanor of the witnesses — well, I am amazed that they can be so disparaging of an honestly reached verdict.

Those two holdout jurors — the ones that didn't go to the Christmas party — simply had a different opinion from the other ten.

• • •

It is perhaps too obvious to mention that all of the principals in the case were archetypes of one sort or another.

- *The pretty Caucasian woman, with an English accent, and her little children, all dressed in white. She even used to be a Jew, but now she is a Catholic. Good soap-opera stuff.*

- *The sadistic German.*

- *The live-in housekeeper-gardener servant couple.*

- *The young Irish gardener, with brogue to match.*

- *Cops, lawyers, judges — all busily doing what cops, lawyers, and judges are paid to do.*

- *Hard-bitten newspaper reporters — even some women — with hearts of mush. We know of one woman by name — Nixola Greeley Smith — but also when we read an article that describes accurately what the defendant was wearing or how she did her hair, we know intuitively that it was written by a woman, a kind of second-string Nelly Bly, as it were. If this is stereotyping, too bad.*

- *The well-meaning nun who gives simply awful advice about family matters.*

- *The well-meaning bishop, ditto.*

• • •

As for Selectman Ryman and his male New Jersey buddies, the less I have to think about them, the better.

• • •

The 19th Amendment to the U.S. Constitution, granting the vote to women, was approved by Congress on June 4, 1919, and was submitted to the States for ratification. In February 1920, the New Jersey Senate ratified it by a vote of 18 to 2 and the Assembly did the same by 34 to 24. After three-fourths of the States gave their OK, the amendment came into effect across the nation on August 18, 1920.

But the right to vote didn't mean that women automatically got the right to sit — or the duty of sitting — on a jury. That was still controversial, and very much fought over, even though women jurors had been called in various courts throughout the country for several years.

And then there is this—

AND HER FIVE LITTLE KIDS ALL DRESSED IN WHITE

Since 1906, New Jersey's Essex County courthouse has been graced by an imposing mural painted by the Ohio artist Kenyon Cox, titled "The Beneficence of the Law" (pictured). In it, three gowned figures present an allegory. One of them, barefoot and ethereal, with the scales of justice, stretches out her hand in judgment over a female monarch on a throne who holds a staff as a symbol of power. Another, seated below them, waits with a sprig of laurel. In one corner three children are playing at the foot of a bare-breasted woman, her lap fecund with fruit, and in another corner two birds are wooing.

Except for the children, all the figures in the mural are women.

One Essex County judge may have been looking at that mural for a long time and, four years after Mrs. Beutinger's acquittal, he perhaps finally realized its unfulfilled meaning.

WOMEN CALLED FOR JURY DUTY

Wednesday, 1/19/1921 (*Edgefield Advertiser*). Last November, Judge Daniel A. Dugan of the Essex County Court in Orange, New Jersey, suddenly found his panel of three hundred male jurors was running out, all the men finding excuses of one kind or another to relieve them of that obligation.

So, being more annoyed than usual, he took the radical step of drafting the newly enfranchised New Jersey women.

The women chosen were carefully picked and represented some of the best families in Orange. Much to the surprise of the Court, they appeared promptly in answering the summons, and none offered an excuse to avoid serving.

At the last moment, it is true. Mrs. Thomas A. Edison telephoned the judge and asked to be excused because her husband was ill, but she said she would find some way to come if he could not find someone else to take her place.

Yes, THAT Thomas A. Edison, the inventor of the light bulb. The couple lived in nearby Menlo Park. Mina Miller Edison (pictured) sounds like an admirable lady.

"We have found women jurors are an unqualified success," Judge Dugan said. "And they have had the effect of making men jurors easier to get. The men seem a little ashamed of themselves, and they are not offering so many excuses to escape serving.

"It is also possible to get a higher type of woman to serve on a jury; the same type of man is too busy to serve.

"Some of the male juries we have are almost feeble-minded, and the verdicts they render are absolutely ridiculous. I have thrown out many verdicts of men juries and ordered retrials. Sometimes I let them stand because it doesn't make any difference anyway. But often the verdicts are too irrelevant to the facts."

The judge is going to try it and see what happens. The panel of three hundred jurors for the Orange court this year is to be made up of 150 men and 150 women. And the next thing he will try is a mixed jury of six men and six women.

The mixed jury, it is believed, will be the most successful kind ever developed under our judicial system.

Judge Dugan then impaneled the first two all-women juries in Essex County.

ALL-WOMAN JURY REACHES VERDICT

Thursday, 10/14/1920 (*New York Tribune*). The first jury of women to ever serve in the Eastern United States returned a verdict after only 35 minutes of deliberation in the district court of Orange, New Jersey.

Judge Daniel A. Dugan, who presided, told the women they had performed their duty excellently. Not one of them tried to avoid service, not one was late, and most of them asked intelligent questions.

The jurors were Marion Knight Garrison, forewoman; Jeannette Mozier, Ruth Glarch, Susan R. Swift, Caroline Dudley, Grace A. Richards, Ella Crawford, Mary Darcy, Annie Munson, Mary Ward, Susan R. Clark, and Catherine Effenberger.

The case was a suit brought by the McCall Pattern Company against Anthony Pascarella, involving payment for $189 worth of patterns.

The jury found in Pascarella's favor.

That was a civil case. The next month the same judge presided over a criminal trial, and—

FIRST ALL-WOMAN CRIMINAL JURY

Thursday, 11/18/1920 (*New York Tribune*). The first jury of women to try a criminal case in Essex County, New Jersey, which includes in its membership Mrs. Thomas A. Edison and Mrs. William A. Lord, wife of the mayor of Orange, New Jersey, will sit with Judge Daniel A. Dugan in the Orange District Court Monday.

They will hear the case of the New Jersey Board of Dentistry against Jack Segal, who is accused of practicing without a license.

The case involved a woman who had suffered through a botched tooth extraction by, yes, someone pretending to be a dentist. That time it took seventeen minutes for the women to reach a verdict. "Guilty."

• • •

Two bronze statues flanked the magnificent stairway entrance of the Essex County courthouse when Mrs. Beutinger

AND HER FIVE LITTLE KIDS ALL DRESSED IN WHITE

was tried in 1916 (as they still do today). The statue of "Truth" (pictured) is a female figure. There is a statue opposite called "Power." It is a man.

• • •

In 1921, New Jersey enacted legislation stating that women would thenceforth be qualified to serve on all juries.

13. Afterword

There is always an Afterword. Stories don't end neatly. Journalists and the public turn their attention to new thrills, new narratives — and yet echoes of the old resound from time to time, as the principals move through their lives — afterward.

Margaret Claire Beutinger's life took some astounding turns.

MRS. BEUTINGER SAYS SHE IS NEAR POVERTY

Sunday, 12/10/1916 (*New York Sun*). When her legal expenses are all paid off, Mrs. Beutinger will be practically penniless, she said yesterday.

She has an equity of $2,500 in the house her husband bought for her last August, where she killed him. Interest on the mortgage, she said, is unpaid, and the holders may foreclose.

The direct costs of her trial have been paid by her sister, Jennie Herron, and other relatives in Jamaica, West Indies.

While she was in jail from July 11 through last Thursday, the home, with her sister and her five children and two servants has been maintained, and the upkeep has nearly exhausted all the resources left by her husband.

"My relatives want me to go back to Jamaica," she declared. "They will provide a home for me and my children. I may go later, but I want to stay and clear up my affairs here."

Despite her financial stress, Mrs. B was resilient. And creative.

KILLER MAY BECOME AUTHOR

Monday, 12/11/1916 (*Trenton Times*). Mrs. Beutinger will strive to make a living for herself and her family through writing.

She has been invited by Alfred Hemming, the father of Violet Fleming, the actress, to collaborate with him in a play. She will also attempt to devote herself to a book of her travels and her experiences.

Theatrical managers have made several tempting offers to her, but she is loath to accept because she refuses to be separated from her children.

Mrs. Beutinger and her oldest daughter, Margaret, attended mass and received communion in St. Aloysius Church, Caldwell, yesterday. After communion, she was visited by a score of well-wishers, including several of the jurors who freed her.

DISMISSES SERVANTS

Tuesday, 12/26/1916 (*New York Sun*). Owing to her straitened circumstances, Mrs. Beutinger has been compelled to dispense with the services of Mr. and Mrs. Eugene Graaf, the gardener and housekeeper who cared for the children during her incarceration.

Since the departure of her faithful servants, both of whom testified at her trials, Mrs. Beutinger admits it is sometimes hard to remain at the house where the tragedy took place.

She says her only means of support are through her children, who will be paid several thousand dollars insurance on their father's life. An administrator has been named by the county to handle the estate, but it is believed that this will amount to practically nothing and that the insurance money is all they will get.

The family's only companion right now is her sister, Mrs. Jennie Herron of Jamaica, West Indies, who expects to remain all winter.

LAWYER SUES FOR FEE

Monday, 5/21/1917 (*New York Tribune*). Margaret Beutinger has been served with papers by Frank M. McDermott, a Newark lawyer, who wants to recover $500 which he claims is due him for services.

Although McDermott did not figure in the case during

the trial, he says his son cashed Mrs. Beutinger's retainer check for $500 in good faith, but the payment was stopped.

Mrs. Beutinger says she was nervous and unstrung when McDermott called on her at the jail on the night of her arrest and offered his services. She stopped payment, she says, on the advice of her counsel, Walter G. Brandley.

We do not know what became of McDermott's claim against her.

We do know, however, what happened when Mrs. B. made a claim on her husband's insurance policy. About what you'd expect: It was denied.

KILLED SPOUSE, LOSES INSURANCE

Monday, 1/7/1918 (*Bridgeport, Connecticut, Telegram*). Margaret C. Beutinger will not be able to collect the $7,500 insurance on the life of her husband.

Judge Duncan, in the Circuit Court at Newark, has decided that the General Accident Life and Fire Insurance Company would not have to pay off on the policy because Christof Beutinger had misrepresented facts on his application: He denied that he indulged to excess in intoxicating liquors. The evidence submitted at the murder trial concerning his mode of life showed that he was a heavy drinker and that he gave way to fits of temper and passion.

And there was also this unfortunate incident:

FORGOT ABOUT AUTO VICTIM

Tuesday, 11/20/1917 (*New York Sun*). Margaret C. Beutinger was arrested Sunday in Montclair, New Jersey, and charged with running down 5-year-old Thomas Meyer and driving on without seeing that he received medical attention.

The victim is in Mountainside Hospital, Glen Ridge, where he was taken by a traffic officer.

Mrs. Beutinger told police that after the accident she was uncertain what course to pursue. She stepped from her machine when a man advised her to rush for a doctor while he would take the boy to a hospital in his car.

Not familiar with Montclair streets, she did not find a doctor, and she began to worry about her own children, who were ill with whooping cough, and she simply forgot about the accident.

LICENSE IS REVOKED

Tuesday, 11/27/1917 (*New York Sun*). Mrs. Beutinger was found guilty of speeding by Motor Vehicle Commissioner Dill in Newark yesterday and her license was revoked.

She was driving an automobile on Bloomfield Avenue in Montclair when she ran down and injured Thomas Meyer, 5.

Witnesses said that Mrs. Beutinger was racing with another automobile at about thirty miles an hour. She denied that she was racing and said she did not know there was another auto alongside her. She claimed that she was not going faster than fifteen miles an hour and that her thoughts were entirely of her children while she was driving.

BURSTS INTO TEARS

Tuesday, 11/26/1917 (*Jersey Journal*). When Commissioner Dill announced that he would find her guilty, she replied that she didn't see "as that amounted to much." He replied that it meant the loss of her license, and she retorted she could get a license in New York. When she was told that she would not be permitted to drive in New Jersey, she burst out crying and begged some consideration.

"You will get the full benefit of the law," Dill said.

SUED FOR DAMAGES

Tuesday, 8/8/1918 (*New York Tribune*). Mrs. Beutinger is the defendant in a $500 civil action suit that begins today in a Montclair, New Jersey, district court. The plaintiff is Thomas A. Meyer Sr., who claims that his son, Thomas Jr., was hurt last spring by an auto that she was driving.

Next, we find that Mrs. Beutinger's troubles with men were not completely over. She was named co-respondent in a suit for separate maintenance, which means that some unhappy woman was accusing her of having had a sexual romp with an errant husband. Separate-maintenance suits were often brought by people, mostly women, who did not believe in divorce but still wanted to live alone and have the other half pay for it.

INTIMATE WITH SUMMER RESIDENT

Friday, 8/19/1918 (*New York Tribune*). Margaret Claire Beutinger, appeared yesterday in the Court of Chancery, Newark, as a co-respondent in a suit for separate maintenance.

The suit was begun by Mrs. Estelle Vander Roest against Dr. Henry Vander Roest, a veterinarian and former president of the Road Horse Association of New Jersey. The Vander Roests are summer residents of Asbury Park.

In the trial before Vice-Chancellor Lane yesterday, Mary E. Vander Roest, the doctor's daughter, testified that she found her father and Mrs. Beutinger together in the dining room of their home late one night last February. Her mother was not at home, having been absent for several days.

Miss Vander Roest testified that her father introduced the woman as "Mrs. Claire." She became suspicious and left her door ajar. Later, she saw her father enter the room that was occupied by the strange woman. She followed him, and a scene ensued.

Mrs. Beutinger took the stand to say that she had returned from New York that night and, feeling ill, had visited a nearby physician, Dr. Alexander K. Roehring. The latter was on the telephone trying to find a night's accommodation for her when Dr. Vander Roest appeared and suggested that he be allowed to take her to his house for the night.

In testimony, Dr. Roehring corroborated that account.

Further testimony will be given Saturday morning by Miss Muriel Ott, who was with Miss Vander Roest when she discovered her father and Mrs. Beutinger together.

NAMED CO-RESPONDENT

Friday, 8/19/1918 (*Trenton Evening Times*). A daughter of Mrs. Vander Roest testified that on February 4 she had found her father and Mrs. Beutinger in a compromising situation. He denied the allegation, testifying that Mrs. Beutinger had been taken ill and he was treating her.

And that was the last we heard about this legal battle, and this man.

• • •

In 1919 Margaret Clair Beutinger copyrighted a song she had written (both words and music) called "The Dawn of Love." The musical arrangement was by the noted composer

William Conrad Polla, the same man who wrote "I'll See You in My Dreams," still popular today among a certain group of aging romantics.

As for the unpaid mortgage on her house in Caldwell—

ARSON SUSPECTED

Saturday, 9/6/1919 (*New Yorker Volkszeitung*). (Translated from the German.) Fire believed caused by arson yesterday destroyed the magnificent home of Mrs. Margaret Clare Beutinger on Hillcrest Road.

It was in this house that she shot her husband in July 1916. The woman was acquitted in her second trial. Mrs Beutinger has lived with their five children in New York for some time.

Why was this story published in a German-language newspaper? Because Mrs. B., though she considered herself "English," had a German last name.

• • •

Within the next few years, Margaret shed Christoph's name and became known as Margaret Rhodes; her occupation was given variously as the president of a coal company or as a "coal broker." She gave the same business address as her husband had used, 1 Broadway in Manhattan.

In 1925 the Rhodeses were living in Pelham, Westchester

AND HER FIVE LITTLE KIDS ALL DRESSED IN WHITE

County, New York. Mother Margaret was age 34, little Margaret, Freddie, Marie and Peter (formerly Christopher Jr. or Charlie) were teenagers, and Billy was 12.

Five years later, the family was in Nassau County, New York. Young Margaret had married Benjamin Linfield, who was living with them. They had a servant, Mary McGowan.

Afterward, it gets weird. Or just as weird, considering all that happened before.

Peter Christopher Rhodes became a journalist. He got his name on a Washington, D.C., list as a supporter in the 1930s of the International Coordinating Committee for Aid to Republican Spain. (The Spanish Republicans were backed by liberals, socialists, and Communists; their opponents, the successful Falangists of dictator Francisco Franco, were the favorites of conservatives, reactionaries, and Nazis.) This meant that after the war Peter Rhodes and many others like him were often "named," as the term went, as suspicious characters just on the verge of treason, if not past it.

Rhodes had been with the federal Office of War Information during World War II. And, sure enough, he was "named" in 1949 by ex-Communist-turned-paid-informer Elizabeth Bentley (one of the most prolific namers of that crowd). She told the FBI with great assurance that Peter had been "involved in giving information to the Soviet government. . . . I learned that he had been born in the Philippine Islands, and there seemed to be some question about his nationality and citizenship inasmuch as his father was reputedly a German citizen."

Then the capper:

"There was also information to the effect that his mother, <u>who in fact was a British intelligence agent</u>, had killed the father during World War I, and thereafter reared Peter herself."

I underline those eight words as typical of the absurd blather of the times, particularly Bentley's blather. But that was happily the final instance that Margaret Clair Beutinger's name appeared adversely in any kind of public document, and the rest of her life was as simple as she had always hoped it would be.

She married a man named Everett Cox and around 1950 moved to Key West, Florida, where she lived quietly for four decades. Socially prominent, she liked gardening, was president of the Key West Women's Club, and founded the Center of Hope, for crippled children.

• • •

Margaret Clair Cox died in Key West on February 9, 1981, at age 93.

Of her five little kids all dressed in white, she was survived by Fred, in New Mexico; William (Billy), in Key West; Margaret O'Brian, in New Jersey, and Marie Morehouse (she of the wet towel), in Connecticut. Peter had died in 1965 in his mother's house, which survivors remembered as a big, beautiful place with a wraparound porch. She had five grandchildren and nine great-grands.

After services at St. Mary's Star of the Sea Catholic Church, Margaret Cox was buried in the Key West City Cemetery.

Chronology

The table shows dates based on interpretation of the available sources, many of them being only approximations.

1875

April 5. Christof Beutinger is born in Heilbron, Germany.

1888

June 14. Margaret Claire Abrahams is born on Jamaica, British West Indies.

1892

Beutinger arrives in the United States and joins the Army, serving until 1913.

1903

December 2. Beutinger becomes a U.S. citizen in Indianapolis, Indiana.

1905, 1909

The Official Register of the United States lists Christof as a clerk in the War Department.

1906-7 and after

Margaret and Christof are married, the place and year not being certain. They live for a brief time in New York City. Then they go to the Philippines. Over the next years, they also travel in other countries, like Germany. Her parents send them money. Christof gambles and engages in graft. She intercedes in Washington, D.C., to save his job so he gets a chance to resign before he is fired.

1908

Little Margaret is born.

1909

Frederick is born.

1910

The couple is separated for a time and live in New York City.

1911

Marie is born. Beutinger is chief clerk, Philippines Division, War Department.

1912

Christopher is born. Also known as Charlie.

1913

February 11. William is born in Philadelphia.

Twins are born in Mount Vernon, New York, but they die.

November. The family sails for Germany, then goes through Russia on their way to the Philippines.

1914

June. The family leaves the Philippines.

Saturday, July 6. Christof is arrested in Honolulu on a charge of beating his wife. He is released the next day. The pair continue to the Mainland, on separate ships. No information as to the whereabouts of the children.

Later in the year. William is born. Also known as Billy or Willy.

They are living in New Rochelle, New York, and quarreling constantly. The children are at school in Hastings-on-Hudson, New York.

Margaret flees her husband to live for a time with the Cummings family in Yonkers, New York.

1915

Monday, January 18. Preliminary decree of divorce granted to Margaret.

Friday, May 7. Divorce decree is final.

Margaret seeks advice from a nun and a bishop, and the couple begins to live together again.

Thursday, December 29. They remarry, in Yonkers, New York.

1916

March. The family moves to Caldwell, New Jersey, because Margaret does not want to live in Mount Vernon, where the twins died.

Wednesday, July 5. Christof visits a German U-boat in Baltimore, returns home late. After dinner, he attempts to make little Margaret and Marie's new dolly stand on her feet. Strikes one of the children. Attacks his wife and injures her eye. The pair begin occupying separate bedrooms.

Thursday, July 6. Margaret visits the Caldwell police chief to complain of brutal treatment by her husband and tells the chief that "something" will happen. The chief says that he cannot interfere in a domestic dispute. Upon her request for a good attorney, he recommends Walter B. Brandley. It is possible that the chief advises her to buy a gun.

Friday, July 7. Margaret visits Starck's drugstore in Caldwell and tells the owner there will soon be "great excitement" in the neighborhood. She asks him where she can find a good lawyer, and the same day she retains Walter Brandley.

Thursday, Friday, or Saturday, July 6, 7, or 8. Margaret orders a revolver.

Sunday, July 9. Christof tries to enter the room where Margaret is sleeping.

Monday, July 10, and Tuesday, July 11. During the day, Margaret receives the revolver delivered by express. She loads it with five bullets. After nightfall, Christof quarrels with her while the older boys are saying their prayers. Three times overnight, he enters the room where Margaret is sleeping. On his third entry, **Margaret shoots him.** She is arrested and taken to the Essex County Jail in Newark. Attorney Frank C. McDermott visits the jail and receives a retainer fee by check.

In the afternoon, a reporter interviews the Beutinger children outside their home in Caldwell.

Wednesday, July 12. Margaret, 8, and Marie, 6, visit their mother in the Essex County Jail. All the children are seen later at their home by a reporter.

Thursday, July 13. A funeral service is held for Christof in the Beutinger home, with interment following in Prospect Hill Cemetery, Caldwell.

Saturday, July 15. It is announced that Margaret has retained Robert H. McCarter as defense attorney and that lawyer Frank C. McDermott has no connection with the case.

Monday, July 24. Margaret makes her first appearance at a preliminary hearing in court before Chief Justice Gummere. Her attorney presents her long affidavit retelling the story of her life and asserting that she shot in self-defense. He asks for bail. The request is denied, and Gummere holds Margaret over for trial in the fall session.

Tuesday, October 24. <u>First trial begins.</u> Jury selected. Prosecution and defense make statements.

Wednesday, October 25. Prosecution presents evidence. Bullets introduced. Nixola Greeley-Smith is in court. Mr and Mrs. Graaf are on the stand. Gardener Cummings is on the stand for the prosecution. The only defense witness is John S. Provost, testifying about the diagram he had drawn.

Thursday, October 26. Margaret testifies. More testimony by Cummings. Other defense testimony is given by Mrs. Julia Cummings, the gardener's aunt; Police Chief Harkey, and three medical doctors. Judge refuses to hear testimony of lawyer Frances H. Donahue concerning religion.

Friday, October 27. Witnesses are Julia Ann (or Anna) Gasco, 15-year-old Austrian servant girl, testifying that Christof tried to molest her, and John H. De Baus, testifying that Christof had offered him money to accuse Margaret of infidelity. Prosecution and defense both rest shortly before 11 a.m., the State offering no rebuttal, but both sides sum up and make their arguments for the jury. Judge Martin charges the jury, which goes into a conference room. Margaret is confident of acquittal and a party is planned for afterward.

Saturday, October 28. Jury asks for more instructions at 9:23 a.m., goes back into the conference room, returns. <u>**Jury reports it cannot agree**</u>, so it is discharged, and Mrs. B. is sent back to jail. She bursts into shrieks as she is led away. It is reported that the jury took two ballots and there were two holdouts who advocated a finding of homicide.

Wednesday, November 8. Ernest Ryman visits Margaret in a cell while on an inspection visit with other freeholders.

Wednesday, November 15. Ryman is arrested on an assault and battery charge, then freed on bail.

Thursday, November 16. The Essex County grand jury is called together by Judge William Martin and told to consider making a charge against Ryman.

Thursday, November 23. By a close vote, the grand jury indicts Ryman for assault and battery.

Friday, November 24. Margaret's children are barred from visiting her when they are brought to the jail by her sister.

Monday, December 4. <u>Second trial begins</u>. Margaret seems like "a new girl." Jury is selected. In his opening statement, prosecutor Newman states Christof was shot from above and that he was not rushing forward. This is a new theory. Police Lieutenant Godfrey is on the stand telling of his tests.

Tuesday, December 5. Prosecution rests. Defense counsel Brandley makes opening statement. Margaret tells her story on the stand and by the end of her testimony is near collapse.

Wednesday, December 6. Prosecution makes an easy cross-examination of Margaret. Two nuns testify for the defense, as does a witness who heard the beating episode in Japan. John H. De Baus also gives his testimony. The defense sums up, and Margaret collapses.

Thursday, December 7. <u>Jury finds Margaret not guilty</u> after a deliberation of three hours and five minutes. Decision rendered at 3:40 p.m.

Monday, December 25. Christmas party.

1917

Monday, February 5. Ryman trial opens.

Wednesday, February 7. Ryman trial ends in a hung jury, rumored eight for acquittal and four for conviction.

Monday, May 21. Margaret has been served with papers claiming she stopped payment on the check given to attorney Frank McDermott for his retainer fee.

Saturday, November 17. Margaret runs down a child while driving and leaves the scene.

Sunday, November 18. She is arrested for failing to render aid to the boy and for speeding.

Monday, November 26. Her driver license is revoked for speeding.

1918

Wednesday, February 6. She spends the night in the home of Henry Vander Roest.

Before Friday, July 19. She is named as co-respondent in a divorce action against Vander Roest.

Thursday, August 8. Trial begins in a damage suit against her stemming from the injury inflicted by her automobile.

1919

Copyrights the words and music to a song, "The Dawn of Love."

Friday, September 5. Fire destroys her home in Caldwell. She and the children are living in New York.

1925

Family is living in Westchester County, New York, under the name of Rhodes.

1930

Family is in Nassau County, New York.

1942

Tuesday, March 24. Margaret's father dies.

1949

Margaret Rhodes is "named" in report to FBI.

Around 1950

Moves to Florida as Margaret Rhodes.

1981

Monday, February 9. Margaret Clair Cox dies.

Credits

Helpful information was received from

- Amber P. at the Newspaper and Current Periodical Reading Room of the Library of Congress.

- KW at the Digital Reference Section of the Library of Congress.

- Elizabeth Parker and Beth Zak-Cohen of the Charles F. Cummings New Jersey Information Center of the Newark Public Library.

- Descendants of Margaret Clair Cox; they provided information for the last chapter.

About the Author

GEORGE GARRIGUES has been a reporter and editor for the *Los Angeles Times* and the head of journalism or communications programs at University of the Pacific, Wayne State University, University of Bridgeport, and Lincoln University of Missouri.

He has also worked on the *Inglewood Daily News* (California), *Ontario Daily Report* (California), *San Francisco Examiner*, *Coast-Valley Journal* (Oregon), Wave Newspapers (Los Angeles), and *Bergen County Record* (New Jersey).

About These Books

CITY DESK PUBLISHING and "Read All About It!" present true stories of the 1890s to the early 1920s as seen in the newspapers of days gone by.

Everything has been edited for your better understanding. To write your high school term paper, doctoral dissertation or Wikipedia article, you will have to check the original sources. All are listed.

To find out more, go to *CityDeskPublishing.com*.

www.ingramcontent.com/pod-product-compliance
Lightning Source LLC
Chambersburg PA
CBHW070237230526
45470CB00002B/444